EMBRACE the WORK, LOVE your CAREER

EMBRACE the WORK, LOVE your CAREER

A GUIDED WORKBOOK FOR REALIZING YOUR CAREER GOALS WITH CLARITY, INTENTION, AND CONFIDENCE

Fran Hauser

BEST-SELLING AUTHOR OF *THE MYTH OF THE NICE GIRL*

ILLUSTRATIONS BY REGINA SHKLOVSKY

THE
collective
BOOK STUDIO

ISBN: 978-1-951412-49-4
LCCN: 2021911391

Printed using Forest Stewardship Council certified stock
from sustainably managed forests.

Manufactured in China

Design by David Miles
Illustrations by Regina Shklovsky

1 3 5 7 9 10 8 6 4 2

The Collective Book Studio®
Oakland, California
www.thecollectivebook.studio

This book belongs to:

Contents

Introduction 1

How to Get the Most Out of This Book 5

Section 1: Fall in Love with Your Career 9

Section 2: Design Your Career Action Plan 29

Section 3: Create Time and Space 73

Section 4: Know Your Value 111

Section 5: Build Your Dream Team 143

Section 6: Reflect and Reset 175

Final Thoughts 194

Love Your Career Tool Kit 197

Acknowledgments 214

About the Author 216

I'm so

happy

YOU'RE HOLDING THIS

book.

Introduction

Throughout my career, I've had the privilege of mentoring hundreds of women—women who were seeking inspiration, clarity, a jolt of confidence, or who simply wanted to confide in someone who's been there and who gets it. Many of these women felt stuck, burned out, or unclear about where to focus their energy. I've also coached women who were in some type of career transition—in between jobs, returning to work, or moving into a different field. What all these smart and capable women had in common was that they wanted (and deserved) to get the most out of their careers.

This book is for them and for you. No matter our age, experience, or background, we all want a career that we love and one that's filled with promise, inspiration, and joy. I believe this is possible. Strike that. It's not only possible; it's powerful and achievable! Through the years, I've used a variety of exercises to help myself and other women achieve this. *Embrace the Work, Love Your Career* holds all of these exercises, along with affirmations and creative space for journaling.

Before we dive into our work together, here's a little bit about me: In 2018, I wrote a book, *The Myth of the Nice Girl: Achieving a Career You Love Without Becoming a Person You Hate*, that's been translated into six languages and was named "Best Business Book of the Year" by Audible. Its core theme is something I love to talk about: that kindness takes strength, strength is kindness, and the best leaders lead with both.

I have spoken at many, many events on this topic, and it was at one of these talks that the idea for a career workbook came to me.

During the question-and-answer session, I was asked about handling self-doubt, and when I shared my favorite confidence-boosting tool, the audience went wild. Well, maybe not *wild*, but I saw enthusiastic nods and that look of hope, that look of possibility. It struck me that, time and again, the advice that resonates the most with my readers is the practical advice—the tips, techniques, and tools. *Tell me how! What steps do I take? How can I integrate these practices into my day?*

I've spent more than twenty years crystallizing this advice—seeing what works and what doesn't—while working in both corporate environments and on my own. I've held leadership roles at big companies such as Coca-Cola Enterprises and Time Inc. and at early-stage companies such as Moviefone. The role that I'm probably best known for is leading the team that relaunched PEOPLE.com and made it one of the largest media websites in the world (as well as one of the most profitable businesses at Time Inc.).

While I enjoyed working at Time Inc., going out on my own to launch my start-up investing practice was one of the best decisions I've ever made. Not only do I love the work, but being my own boss gives me the opportunity to have more time for my family.

I've invested in more than twenty-five female-founded companies across consumer packaged goods, media, and wellness, and I've found many similarities between mentoring female founders and mentoring women in the workplace. Their needs and pain points are the same: they all have an endless list of to-dos but are running in place, they often feel as if they don't belong or deserve a seat at the table, and they have a hard time getting out of the weeds.

As I embarked on creating *Embrace the Work, Love Your Career*, my vision was to create a book that you'll want to spend time with and that will help you move through your career with clarity, intention, and confidence. Through simple, inspiring, and actionable tools, you'll be empowered to focus on the things that truly matter, set boundaries, and, ultimately, realize your full potential.

Achieving a career you love takes work. So let's dig in and do the work.

I'm excited to be going on this journey with you!

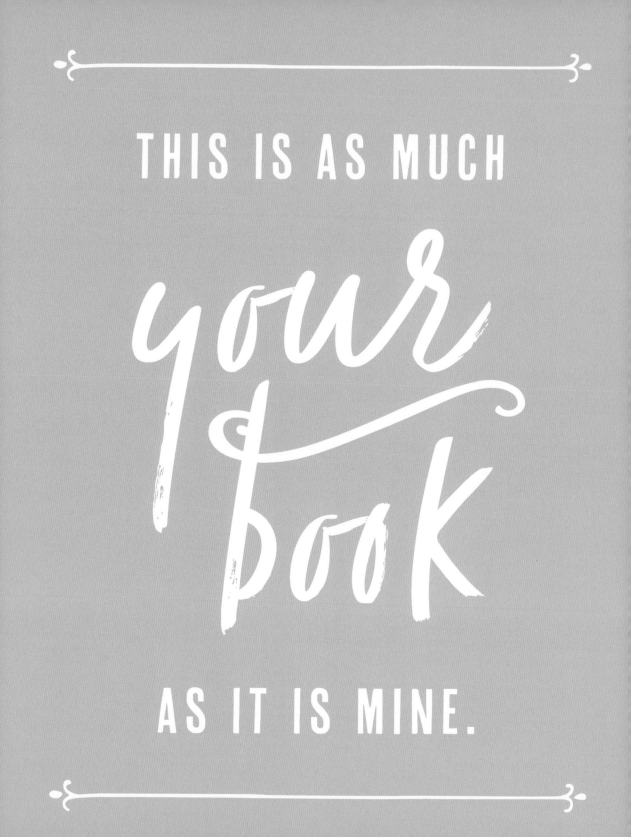

How to Get the Most Out of This Book

This is as much *your* book as it is *mine*. My intention is for it to be highly interactive so you can make it your own. You will find everything from creative prompts and thought starters to affirmations and meditations that will help you stay present. It even includes coloring breaks to reinvigorate your creative juices.

The fundamental premise of this book is that if you want to love your career, you need to embrace the work. The work is ongoing; it's made up of regular practices and check-ins that will enable you to create a career you love. And the work starts with this book.

It's organized into six sections:

Section 1: Fall in Love with Your Career. *We'll start by taking an airplane view of your career and envisioning what would make you love it.*

Section 2: Design Your Career Action Plan. *In this section, we will establish four clear, focused goals that will actualize your career vision. This is the biggest section and your guidepost for the whole book.*

Section 3: Create Time and Space. *To set yourself up for success in attaining those goals, you'll learn healthy practices and exercises to set boundaries so that you have the time and space to focus on the work that matters.*

Section 4: Know Your Value. *Goals are difficult to achieve if you're lacking the self-assurance to do so. Here's where we tackle the inner work that allows you to lean into your strengths.*

Section 5: Build Your Dream Team. *Everyone needs a dream team or support network that includes people who can serve as a sounding board, open doors, and give encouragement when you need it. In this section, we will work on assembling yours.*

Section 6: Reflect and Reset. *In this final section, you'll discover how mindfulness can help you move through your career (and achieve those goals!) with clarity, intention, and confidence.*

Feel free to choose your own path; jump around among the different sections and go right to the topics that are most relevant for you. If starting with the big-picture thinking of sections 1 and 2 feels overwhelming, go right to section 3 and start clearing out your to-do list. At the same time, I do believe that you will get the most out of the book by reading it in its entirety. Here are five more ways to get the most out of this book:

1. **Just write.** *I know how thrilling, scary, inspiring, and thought-provoking it can be to take the time to reflect on your career. Lean into all those emotions. Trust your gut. As you approach the exercises throughout the book, let go of the need to write down neat, concise thoughts, or what you think you should be saying. Write down what you really want to say, even if it's shocking or unexpected! The process of writing has been proven to help you remember things better and feel more connected to the words. Enjoy the process and what you may discover along the way.*

2. **Don't feel that you have to do every single exercise.** *If you feel that an exercise doesn't relate to you or it's just too tough, skip it. The goal of this book is to provide thought starters to unpeel the layers of your career. It's designed to help you, not create more stress!*

Take time to reset. *At the end of every section, you'll find a coloring page to provide relaxation and an original meditation courtesy of my dear friend and mindfulness advisor, Patricia Karpas. Even if you've never meditated, read through these short reflections designed to inspire you. I've found that taking a pause to reflect, even for just a minute, puts me in the right mindset to create intentions for the changes I'd like to make. Give it a try; trust me. You can also use the QR code at the end of each meditation to listen to the audio version.*

Create a peer group. *If you learn better with a support circle, consider going through the book with a group of close colleagues or friends. You can create your own mentor circle and support and challenge each other along the way.*

Keep coming back to it. *My hope is that this book becomes your career companion and that you integrate it into your every day at work. Life is fluid. Goals change, so careers do too! This is not a one-and-done process; feel free to cross things out, use a highlighter—the messier, the better.*

I'm so excited for you to make this book your own and create a career you love!

Fall in Love with Your Career

L et's get started by taking an airplane view of your professional life. When was the last time you stepped back and asked yourself, "Am I loving what I'm doing? What makes me happy about my job? What doesn't?" Yes, we all talk about work *a lot*, but we often don't ask ourselves the right questions— the tough questions. This kind of self-assessment and reflection can repower your career. Falling in love with your career *is* possible, and this book breaks down the process into manageable, achievable steps with guided questions that will leave you feeling as if you can conquer the world—or at least the workplace. Are you ready to give yourself time and space to check in with yourself and your career? Let's go!

What Would Make You Love Your Career?

I recently spoke with my friend Joy about her career path. She told me that in college she focused on preparing for her dream job: retail buying. She majored in it, worked retail on the weekends, and landed a job as an assistant buyer at Macy's. Pretty quickly, Joy realized how unequipped she was for the reality of the job—90 percent of it was math—and Joy admitted she was really bad at math. She had to run reports every Monday, and it took her twice as long as other assistants to do her job. She would go into the office every Sunday to get ahead of it just so she could fight the Sunday scaries.

But Joy also found a few bright spots. She made a lot of friends and was always asked for advice on how to communicate better. She also ended up being the welcome buddy to every new hire. One day, Joy's boss pulled her aside and said, "You seem more like a people person than a numbers person. What would you think about a job in HR?" Joy realized her boss was completely right. She transferred to human resources and began a fifteen-year career where her passion and strengths aligned. It was truly a dream job.

Not everyone is as fortunate as Joy to have a manager or mentor help guide them toward the right career path. Often, it requires a bit of self-reflection and soul-searching. That's where this book comes in. It's easy to lose focus on the big picture when you are in the day-to-day of your life, mired in to-dos. For most of us, career growth takes a back seat to the urgency of getting through your workload. But your career is so much more than your job, so carving out time for reflection and planning is critical if you ever want to pick your head up from your desk and focus on doing more of what you love.

Together we will focus on what would make you love your career *today* because investing in it now can set you up to love it in one, five, or ten years.

I've been doing my own introspection and thinking about why I love my career. I've come to this: I love my career because I enjoy the work, I'm good at what I do, I'm making an impact, I feel valued, and it fits with the rest of my life.

It took me a lot of time to come up with that sentence. But I have more than twenty-five years of a career—filled with setbacks and successes, lows and highs, confusion and clarity—from which to draw. Still, answering the question, "What would make you love your career?" isn't easy. But one constant I've discovered is that people who say they love their careers tend to be doing work that checks most of these boxes:

- ◯ *They want a career they enjoy.*
- ◯ *They want to be good at it.*
- ◯ *They would like their career to make an impact.*
- ◯ *And they want to feel valued while doing it.*

Over the next several pages, I have a series of questions to help you begin to reflect on each one of these points. By the end of this exercise you *will* have more clarity on what you enjoy doing, what you wish you were doing more of, and the aspects of your work that are not serving you well, so you can move forward with purpose. Take notes and jot down ideas where it makes sense. Nothing needs

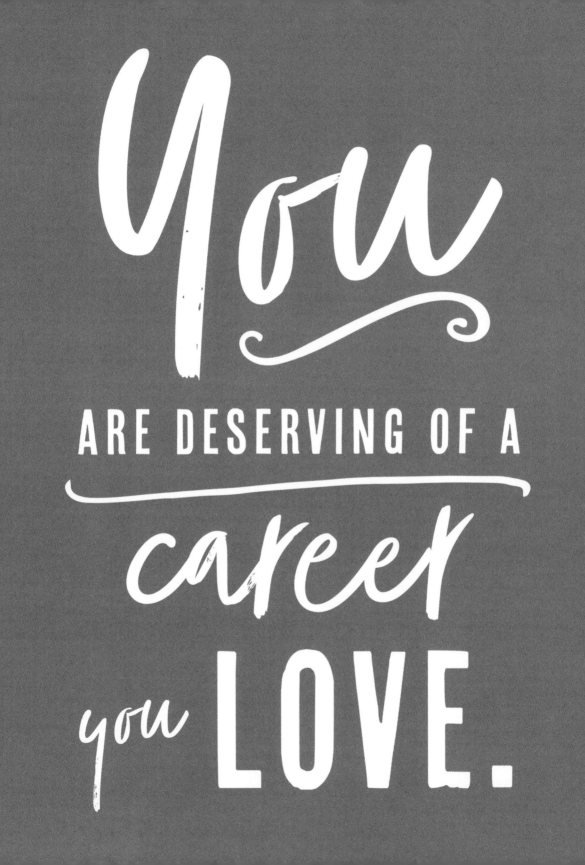

to be perfect. This is free-form. You can always come back to this section (and you should!). Above all: think big, be bold, be truthful. These reflections will be your North Star when it's time to create your career action plan.

ENJOYING THE WORK

What aspects of your most recent job did you (or do you) love and want to do more of?

Look back at your work calendar for the last three months and highlight the meetings/conversations that bring a smile to your face. What are the aspects of those interactions that made you happy? Were they the topics you were discussing, the work you were doing, or the individual/team you were meeting with?

What aspects of your most recent job did you (or do you) dread?

DOING WORK THAT I'M GOOD AT

What are you good at doing? Which parts of your job come easily to you?

_____

_____

_____

_____

Which parts of your job do you find really difficult and stressful?

_____

_____

_____

_____

MAKING AN IMPACT

Which projects or tasks do you feel create the most value for your team, your boss, your company, maybe even the world?! Which ones make you most proud?

FEELING VALUED

In what ways do you feel most appreciated for the work that you do? This could be anything from feeling as if you're fairly compensated to receiving positive feedback on a specific project.

Hopefully, this type of introspection can help you visualize the building blocks of a career that you could fall in love with. If nothing else, it can help pinpoint what you enjoy doing, what you wish you were doing more of, and the things that are not serving you well.

So, what would make YOU love YOUR career?

Creative Workspace

Use this space to combine your insights into a career vision statement or make a career bucket list. Write it out or draw your vision. There are no rules! If you're really stuck, think back to when you were a child: What are the things you loved to do? Did you love to read, tell stories, play on a team? Use all of that for inspiration.

Let this page serve as your North Star to guide the planning you will be doing in the next section!

Pause and Reflect

Y ou did it! Going through this section and reflecting on what's working (and what's not) is a really important first step in creating a plan to love your career. Remember, nothing is set in stone. You can always revisit your thoughts and ideas. My intention is to help you create room to grow, whether you're looking to get out of a rut or happy in your career but looking for more. Remember to reset after each section by enjoying the meditations and mandalas. Reflection leads to clarity, and clarity leads to action. That's next.

Meditation

Start by finding a comfortable seat. Take a moment to connect with your breath.

Having an open heart and an open mind allows us to wonder—to be curious with a growth mindset.

Instead of defaulting to mindless acceptance of the way things are, as if on autopilot, try reflecting on this question: "I wonder if there is another way?" "I wonder if I could let go of some of the work that drains me and do more of the work that I love?"

When we become preoccupied with what we believe others expect, we may lose sight of what matters most to us. Instead, practice listening to what is real for you. Reflect on your own values, on what is meaningful for you. This soul-searching will help you clarify what you love most about your career and visualize the things that bring you more joy every day.

Stop and listen to yourself. Trust yourself.

Imagine a career that is rewarding. Envision a career where you enjoy the work that you're doing, where you feel valued, and where you are making an impact. How does it feel?

When you believe wholeheartedly in your vision, you will inspire the intention, attitude, and action to do everything in your power to make that vision a reality.

When we open our hearts and minds, we can more clearly see the incredible things that are possible for us.

 If you would prefer to listen to the meditation, scan the QR code or visit franhauser.com/loveyourcareer.

Musings, Downloads, and Doodles

Design Your Career Action Plan

Section 1 was about reflecting on how you feel about your career and what would help you love it more. Now, it's time to do the work to make it a reality. In this section, we will work together to identify a few key goals that will set you up for a fulfilling career while also making you more valuable at work. These goals will be game changers and are the key ingredients of your career action plan. Let's craft them.

Set Your RBGS

Most people don't have a hard time setting goals. In fact, many of us have a laundry list of them. The challenge comes in creating goals that are grounded in purpose and will help you design a career you love. Enter: your really big goals (RBGs).

RBGs are different from everyday goals because they are the ones that are going to have the biggest impact on your career. They're also action-oriented and very specific. "Getting a promotion" is a fine goal, but "becoming an expert in search engine optimization" (which will lead to a promotion) is strategic, purposeful, and clear. It's an RBG. RBGs are super important and are key to helping you focus on actions that are going to help move your career forward and—most important—in the direction that's right for you.

For me, when I've focused on and set RBGs in the following four areas, I have experienced an outsized impact on my career:

1. *Value creation: doing things that create true value for my company or organization*

2. *Connections: growing and cultivating mutually beneficial relationships*

3. *Skills: leveling up on fundamental skills and ones that offer new opportunities*

4. *Brand: being intentional about what I want to be known for*

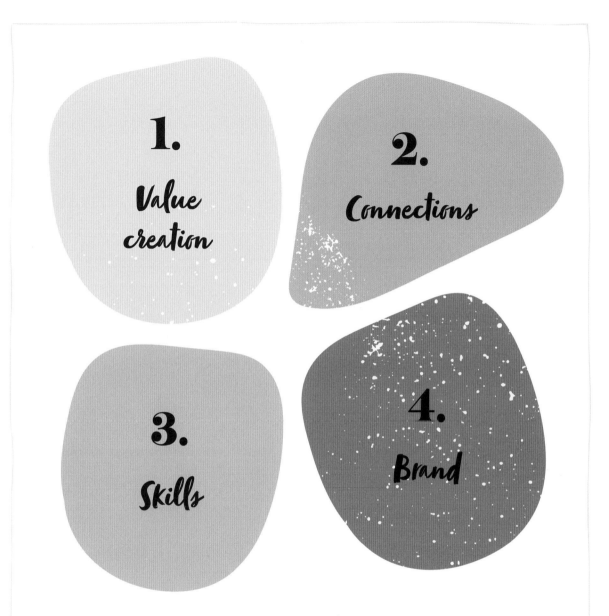

1. Value creation

2. Connections

3. Skills

4. Brand

The next step on the journey to loving your career is to identify your RBGs. When you establish RBGs for each of these areas, you add intention and purpose to your actions. I have a series of fun, thought-provoking exercises to help you identify one new RBG in each area. I suggest just one to help you stay focused. Let's get started!

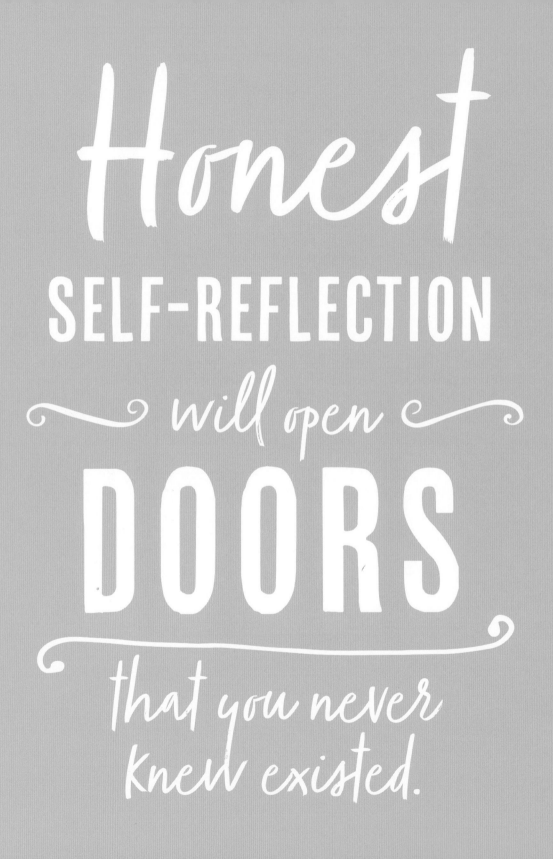

VALUE CREATION

Loving your career is hard to do if you're not creating real value at work. Consider the question: "How can you become indispensable in your job?" If I could use only two words to answer that question, my answer would be: "Create value." Two very simple, yet powerful, words.

Yet it's so easy to get consumed in your day-to-day work and mile-long to-do list. It happens to me all the time. And I often need to remind myself to stop and ask, "Is the work I'm doing creating real value for the company?" And by *value*, I mean, the kind of value that is visible and people talk about. The kind of value that makes me proud and confident.

My friend Beth was always the first person to raise her hand and volunteer to stay late. She worked heads-down hard, but it became clear after she was passed over for a promotion that her work was invisible. What was missing from her to-do list was a meaty project that drove real value for her company. When you create value for your organization, it unlocks new opportunities for your career, whether you want to continue to grow at your company or you're interested in moving in a different direction. This is especially true when you have something tangible that you can talk about or when others can clearly see the impact of your work.

Consider these four fundamental ways to add value to a company: increase revenue, decrease costs, enhance the culture so it's more productive, or develop a breakthrough (a new product, process, or

Revenue

Increase it.

Costs

Decrease them / find efficiencies.

Four Ways to Create Value at Work

Culture

Make it more productive and inclusive.

Breakthrough

Develop a new product, process, or model.

business model) that usually has longer-term impact. How do you know whether your idea or RBG is a value creator? I often use this lens to determine whether what I'm doing is truly creating value: If it checks one of these boxes, then I know that I'm on the right track.

Ultimately, being a value creator is being known for something important that you contributed to or accomplished. Very early on in my career, I was working at Coca-Cola Enterprises in the finance department. My boss asked me if I would work with him to update the format of our quarterly financial report, which was long and hard to digest. And each report was sent to very busy people (our board of directors and senior management!). We ended up shrinking the report to a small, easy-to-read pamphlet that provided the important takeaways. I ended up winning an award for this work, and this is a great example of what it means to do visible work that creates value. I also realized that I was good at simplifying complicated things, which became a part of my brand and what I was known for. The way others perceive you (i.e., your brand) can have a direct impact on your success. (We explore this on page 56.) This project, along with other value-creating projects, ultimately resulted in a big promotion for me—at age twenty-seven—that had me leading a team of 140 people.

Let's now work on *your* value-creation RBG. (Note: If you're in between jobs, skip to page 42 to brainstorm ways to create value while in transition.) Although you may not know the answers to some of these questions and you may have to go on a little bit of a fact-finding mission, be curious and open. Listen actively. Roll up your sleeves and dig in!

What are your company's biggest goals and how can you have a direct impact on them? Some companies are great at communicating their goals; others not so much. If you're clear on what they are, great. Write them down here and consider ways your work can impact these goals. If not, work with your manager to develop a specific goal for you that would benefit the company. If you're stuck, refer back to the four ways to create value on page 34.

Goals (Company, Boss, or Team)	How You Can Contribute

Is there a high-profile project that you would like to be a part of? You know, those projects that everyone is talking about? Make your case for why you would be a good fit for the team working on one of them and share the strengths you bring to the table. If you don't ask, the answer is always "No."

Do you see a new business opportunity that you can pitch to your manager? For example, is there a new market or trend to capitalize on or a potential partnership that can accelerate growth? Do you have ideas about a breakthrough product or a new business model?

Is there a way for the company/your department/your team to be more efficient? Do you have an idea that would reduce costs? Maybe it's changing a process in your current role, using new technologies to automate "spreadsheet systems," or renegotiating vendor terms. This could be an actual reduction in costs or streamlining processes so that employees are more productive and have greater output.

When you look back at your notes, is there one project that stands out? Is there a project that you know will add value to the company and is in line with your career vision?

🖉 **Based on these insights, write your value creation RBG here.**

(Example: "To overhaul our onboarding process to create a more inclusive and welcoming experience for new hires.")

Once you have identified your RBG, think about your next steps. What is the first thing you can do to move to action? Is there someone you need to talk to (your manager, perhaps?) or research to do? Jot down some ideas and star one next step that can activate your RBG.

On page 64, you'll find space to capture all your RBGs in one place in your Career Action Plan. Add your Value Creation RBG and the first next step there.

How do you create value if you're in between jobs?

When my niece Sophie graduated from the University of Miami (with high honors in data analytics) in May 2020, it was challenging to find a job related to her major. When she saw she was going to have to press "pause" on the job search until the world started to recover from the pandemic, she decided to pursue a few "side hustles" that would keep her engaged and generate income. She launched what became a very successful cheese board business called @boardsbysoph, took on social media management for others (including my bookstagram), and tutored high school students in math. All of these experiences contributed to her growth and, frankly, gave her something interesting to talk about when her job interviews picked up again. She also met some really interesting people who opened doors for her. It took a lot of confidence, discipline, and a positive attitude to say, "Well, things didn't quite go as planned, so what am I going to do about it?"

If you're currently in transition, I know it can be hard to find good projects, let alone be strategic about choosing them. I also know that some of the best opportunities arose for friends of mine much later than they expected. Be patient, when possible, and keep fueling your passion. Start by brainstorming a project wish list. Write every idea that comes to mind that you would either love to work on or want to get started on. These could be volunteer projects, too. My friend Michelle worked for the United Way when she was in transition, and it was a wonderful way to build meaningful connections and skills while also feeling valued and purposeful. How would you most like to spend your time? Which projects would make you feel the happiest and most satisfied? Which would be best to talk about in a job interview?

Use this space to jot down some thoughts.

YOUR CONNECTIONS

Your network is your lifeline. Building relationships and connecting with people is one of the most important ways to invest in yourself and your career.

When I talk to fellow senior leaders, most of them say they wouldn't be where they are today without their incredible networks. These are all highly intelligent, hardworking people who realized that stepping away from the computer, broadening horizons, and taking the time to meet new people can help your job, too. It's really hard to change a career or to grow in your own industry without a network of people to open doors for you. And the things you learn from others while you're out networking can benefit you *and* your company.

Connecting is also about building mutually beneficial relationships that can assist you down the road. I know I wouldn't have been able to pivot from media to investing without my network.

One example of this happened in the spring of 2013. I was sitting outside the Time-Life Building, having coffee with my friend and start-up founder, Soraya Darabi. I often met with founders to discuss potential partnership opportunities with our brands, like *PEOPLE* and *InStyle*. On an otherwise run-of-the-mill day, Soraya said something that would change the trajectory of my career. "Fran, there are so many women who are looking to launch businesses," she said, "and when they look up, they don't have any female role

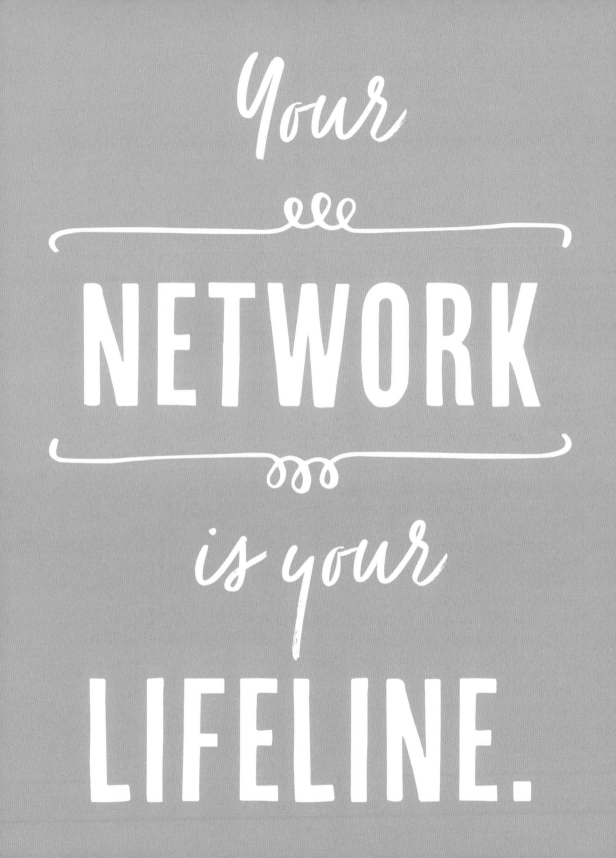

models or mentors, and you could be that." With that, Soraya planted the seed of vision for me.

So I tested the waters by investing in and advising a few digital media start-ups while I was still at Time Inc. I quickly realized that this side hustle could become my full-time thing: I had the network and plenty of deal flow, and I was really enjoying it.

This wasn't just a happy coincidence. Prior to that coffee date, I realized that what I loved about my work was emerging technology and nonprofit opportunities. But when I looked at my network, it consisted of mostly (wonderful) media people. I wanted to learn more outside my industry, so I became strategic about seeking connections in those two sought-after spaces. You can do this, too. Depending on where you want to go in your career, you may need to build out different types of networks. (If you want to read more about my networking strategies, I wrote extensively about this in *The Myth of the Nice Girl*. It's chapter 7.)

What is your higher-level vision in building out your network?

Think back to what you stated would help you love your career. How can connections help you get there? Your connections RBG is going to look very different if you want to accelerate your career within your company versus outside of your company. What's your WHY when it comes to meeting new people and making connections? Is it:

- ○ *to find senior-level mentors at your company?*
- ○ *to learn more about a new industry/space?*
- ○ *to build a side hustle?*
- ○ *to find peer mentors who you can learn from and lean on?*

It could be a combination of these or something else.

Write it here!

_____

_____

_____

_____

What are you hoping to learn or gain from these new relationships?

_____

_____

_____

_____

*✎ **Based on these insights, write your connections RBG here.***

(Example: "To meet ten new people this year who can help me learn more about content marketing at a consumer packaged goods company and make introductions so that I can eventually break into that industry.")

Once you have identified your RBG, think about who you could reach out to and organizations that host events that could align with your goals. Jot down some ideas and star one next step that can activate your RBG.

Add your Connections RBG/next step to your Career Action Plan on page 64.

You
have the power
TO CREATE YOUR OWN
opportunities.

YOUR SKILLS

Skills can be built in the natural course of your work. The more you do something, the better you get at it. But there may be skills that you need to build outside of your work. Perhaps you're working in marketing, and there is a new social media platform that you are not assigned to, but you know it's important for your career that you learn how to use it for brand building and sales. I remember very early on in my career when I was working in finance and accounting, activity-based costing became all the rage. Because companies often do things the way they've always done them, it wasn't in my purview to learn this new skill, so I had to be proactive and learn it on my own. But even taking that kind of initiative can have an upside as it can create an opportunity to take a leadership role in introducing new technologies and processes to the company.

What are the skills that you would like to invest in?

Start with where the opportunity is out in the world. Many resources available online report on the most valuable career skills based on industry and market trends. In recent years, some of the things on the list could be: tech skills like Python and React, data analysis, performance marketing, and health care/wellness solutions. Talking to people you respect (both inside and outside of your company) is also a good way to gather data. I always say make friends with recruiters and grab a coffee with them once in a while. They have a wealth of knowledge when it comes to where the heat is in the market. Jot down these new career skills in the following table.

Then, think about essential skills you could improve on. Maybe they're soft skills like being a good listener or creating trust among team members; maybe they're fundamental skills for your job like public speaking or being a spreadsheet wizard. Also note these in the following table.

For each skill, ask yourself two questions: Is the skill aligned with the career vision you laid out in section 1, and do you think you can be good at it? There are some things that—no matter how hard I try—are really difficult for me to learn, and it's not worth investing my time. For example, creating graphics for social media content takes me *forever*. I was wasting so much time trying to get the right look. I ultimately decided to hire an awesome intern to help me with this, and it's been life changing. It leaves me time to focus on what I am good at. It's important to be honest with yourself when you are doing this assessment.

Potential Skills to Invest In	Is the skill aligned with the career vision you laid out in section 1?	Do you think you can be good at it?
	☐	☐
	☐	☐
	☐	☐
	☐	☐
	☐	☐
	☐	☐
	☐	☐
	☐	☐

Based on this exercise, think about what would be most helpful in making your career vision a reality. Can you pick one skill that you would like to focus on first?

Write your skills RBG here.

(Examples: "To learn how to create and leverage a LinkedIn newsletter to attract new customers" or "To be a more inclusive manager by learning how to give better feedback and support all the members of my team.")

Once you have identified your skill, think about ways you can level up or master the material. Are there online courses you can take (LinkedIn Learning, General Assembly, etc.), are there books you can read, is there a networking group you can join, or are there experts in your network that you can learn from? Jot down some ideas. Star one next step that can activate your RBG.

Add your Skills RBG/next step to your Career Action Plan on page 64.

YOUR BRAND

We all have people in our lives who we go to for specific things. I lean on my friend Emily for social media insights and inspiration; when I am evaluating an investment opportunity, I often talk to my friends Annie and Janna. These friends have become invaluable to me in those specific areas. That is their capital.

Becoming a go-to on a topic (aka branding yourself) increases your visibility and desirability—it can help make you indispensable. Admittedly, *branding* is an overused word, but identifying a brand RBG for your career will inspire you to think about what you want to be known for or what makes you a sought-after employee. So how do you become a go-to? You tap into your natural skill set or passion and look for opportunities at your company to hone, share, and develop your unique knowledge and perspective. There is no brand without substance.

When Time Inc. launched an initiative called Time Inc. University, they put a call out to internal leaders to pitch course ideas. The topics ranged from photography to reading a financial statement, and it gave us a chance to brand our expertise. (I signed up to teach how to build a digital business.)

Do you have a skill/secret sauce that you can package and train others on? Some companies have a formal training program that you could volunteer for, but you could also start an informal Lunch and

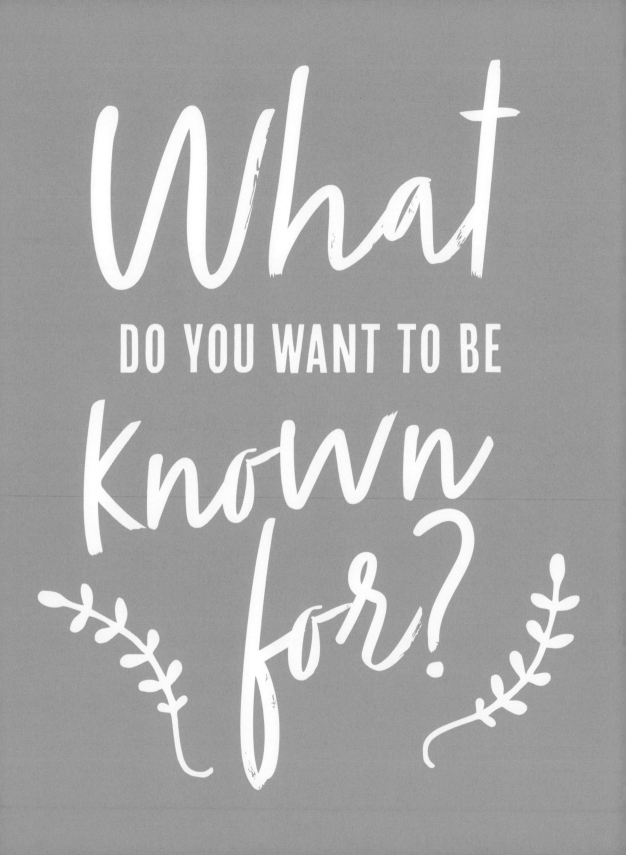

Learn with four or five other employees where each of you brings a lesson to share.

If you want to reach even more people, consider creating, curating, or sharing on social media or another digital platform whatever it is you're passionate about. I met a young woman at Uber who shares fun reels on Instagram showing the behaviors that hold women back at work. They are engaging and smart and, by doing this, she is building her reputation as someone who cares about career building and equality at work. Likewise, I got my first book deal for *The Myth of the Nice Girl* because of a blog post I wrote for *Forbes* on "Nice Girls Finishing First." Leading with both kindness and strength is what I became known for in my career, and I felt that I had expertise to share. If this sounds like fun to you, pick a platform (it can be blogging, Instagram, even Twitter) and just start. See what resonates with people. Have fun with it. You never know where this might lead.

What do you want to be known for?

First, think about where your passions lie or what you love learning about. What talents come naturally to you? What interests you that you want to share with the world? It could be something that on the surface seems not work-related, like fitness hacks or book reviews; it could also be a topic that fires you up, like diversity and inclusion or mental health at work. It also could be something values-driven, such as being known for kind leadership or radical candor.

Use this space to capture some ideas.

Now, let's edit the list. Think back to your vision and what would make you love your career. What concepts or topics that you wrote about above speak to that vision? For example, if you're thinking about transitioning to a career in project management, being a go-to for productivity hacks would be a natural fit. Pick one topic or idea that you can own.

Write your brand RBG here.

(Examples: "I want to be known for my ability to coach others" or "I want to be an expert on pay equity at work.")

How can you start to establish yourself as the go-to on this topic? Can you start training others? Write about it? Curate your social media platform? This is not meant to stress you out or add another groan-worthy to-do to your list. Instead, think of this as an opportunity to create your own narrative. Star the go-to item that would be the best next step.

Add your Brand RBG/next step to your Career Action Plan (see page 64).

Before we review your Career Action Plan on page 64, I want to take a minute to say it's okay if you don't have all your RBGs completely crystallized. This section may take more digging, reflecting, and questioning. The great news is that you can continue working on the rest of the sections in parallel with developing your RBGs. Or you can get through the rest of the book and then come back to this section.

Alternatively, you might be in a position where you have all four RBGs identified but are feeling overwhelmed. You don't have to do all four at the same time. They're really big goals, after all! You might want to start by focusing on connections and skills or value creation and brand. This is YOUR plan. Even if you pick one area to start, this should feel satisfying, gratifying, and clarifying. I know that's a lot of -ings, but when you have an action plan and can see your RBGs on one page, it won't feel like work; it will feel like progress.

And know that this is not set in stone. You can always revisit, update, and change your RBGs. It's a fluid process. You may start down one path before the light bulb flashes. There is beauty in the process of achieving, failing, and resetting. This is your career to own, to envision, to love.

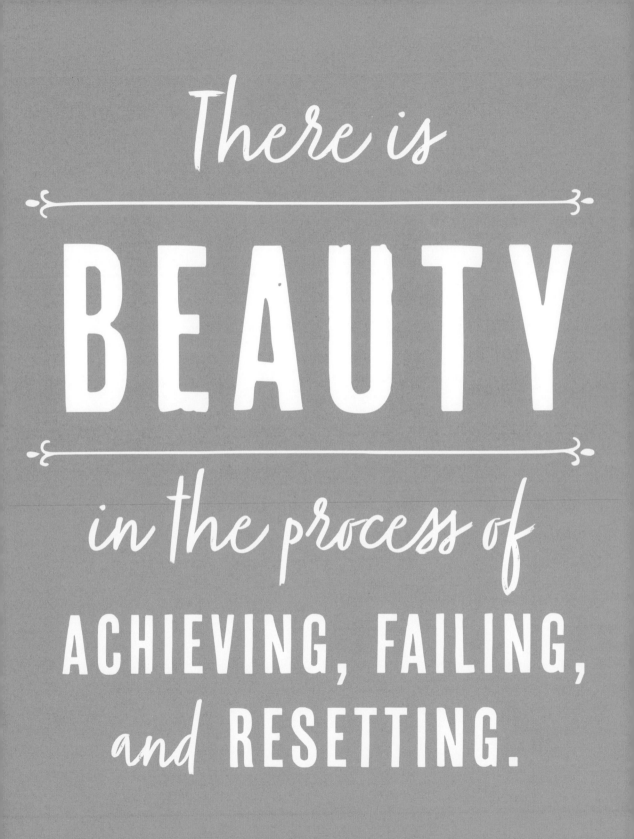

There is

BEAUTY

in the process of

ACHIEVING, FAILING,
and RESETTING.

Career Action Plan

Area	RBG	Next Step
Value Creation		
Connections		
Skills		
Brand		

ACTIVATING YOUR CAREER ACTION PLAN

1 Add your next steps to your calendar/to-do list

2 Take a photo of your plan, post it on your bulletin board, add it to your phone notes— whatever works for you!

3 You will find extra pages in the back of the book. If you prefer a digital download, visit franhauser.com/loveyourcareer.

Pause and Reflect

I hope that you feel great about the investment you've made in mapping out your Career Action Plan. You've answered tough questions, done some soul-searching, and made hard decisions. Embrace your progress!

Now you might be thinking, "How am I going to make room for these new goals with everything else on my plate?" In the next section, we are going to work on that . . . creating time and space so that you can prioritize the work that truly matters.

Meditation

Find a comfortable spot where you can be relaxed and alert at the same time. Bring your attention to your breath and follow it with each inhale and exhale. This will anchor you. This is a time for you to be still, to reflect on what is most important to you.

Take a moment to imagine yourself in a rewarding career. What thoughts and emotions arise as you imagine yourself doing what you love?

Now, imagine what it would take to be in this career. How would you prepare yourself? Are you showing up in a way that is authentic to your values? What do you want to be known for?

Stepping out of our comfort zones and our day-to-day routines inspires us to open our eyes to new and unexpected opportunities. What will you do differently? How will you invest in yourself?

Now, as we close this meditation, take a moment to focus your attention back on your breath. Use this as a reminder to invest your time and awareness on the things that matter most.

Take this idea with you wherever you go.

 If you would prefer to listen to the meditation, scan the QR code or visit franhauser.com/loveyourcareer.

Musings, Downloads, and Doodles

Create Time and Space

N ow that you have your RBGs, let's create time so that you can fit them into your calendar. Impossible? Not quite. I know how daunting a to-do list can be, and there have been countless times over the course of my life when I took one look at mine and felt completely paralyzed. The key to feeling more in control of your time is recognizing that you have the power to choose (or, at a minimum, influence) where you are going to spend it. By the end of this section, you'll say hello to an upgraded to-do list and more space to love your career!

Create time

IN YOUR DAY FOR THE THINGS

THAT MATTER OR BRING YOU

Joy.

Three Ways to Create Time

Think about the last time you had a really productive day where you made a number of important decisions, crossed off key to-dos, and reached out to a few new connections. That felt good, right? Now think about a day when you felt as if you got nothing meaningful done. Maybe you were sending out "next steps" after a series of back-to-back meetings, spent half the day listening to your coworkers vent, or were researching icebreakers for meetings instead of industry trends. At the end of that day, you're not sure what you accomplished, but you certainly felt very busy doing it.

You had the same amount of hours on both of these days, but the difference lies in what made you feel accomplished. In one, you were in control and crossed off tasks that had a bigger impact on your company or career. In the other, unexpected distractions and assignments took up much of your attention. One day felt active; the other passive. That's what we are going to do in this section: take action to create more time and space for your RBGs.

I can't create more hours in the day (as much as we would all love that), but I have a plan to help you get stuff off of your current to-do list, including a framework for (kindly) saying "No" to future requests that are not aligned with where you want to and need to spend your time. Finally, we will cover some behaviors that can help you change the way you work to create more bandwidth. When we get through this work together, I promise you will be able to get your RBGs in!

Three Ways to Create Time

1

Take stuff off your list.

2

Say "No" (to keep stuff off your list).

3

Change the way you work.

TAKE STUFF OFF YOUR LIST

There's a reason our to-do lists are overloaded: We rarely take the time to purge them! Every year (or twice a year), attack this step as you would a closet clean-out, assessing what really needs to be on the list and what you need to let go. I did this with my friend Maria, who was struggling with feeling as if she never had enough time in the day. I asked her to take me through how she was spending her days and which projects or tasks were the most time-consuming, not just at work but across her life. She mentioned a school task force that she had been sitting on for a few years and was devoting around ten hours per week to it. I asked her if that work was rewarding or helping to deliver on any of her RBGs. She said it was at one point in time, but that she was now doing it only because she felt guilty leaving the task force. Ding! A sign that this could be a place to free up some time.

We talked through how she could leave the project and feel good about the way she left. I encouraged her to start the conversation by letting the project organizers know how much this work has meant to her and how grateful she was to have been a part of it and that it was time for her to move on but she would love to leave the door open. I also asked her to think about some low-lift ways in which she could continue to be helpful. She said she would be happy to continue donating to the annual fundraiser and helping spread the word through social media. She felt good about leaving in this way and had now found an extra ten hours a week to devote to her RBGs.

Create a to-don't list

Look at your work calendar and to-do lists for the last three months. Is there anything that stands out to you as unnecessary? Are there things you do just because you've always done them? As you look at each task or meeting, ask yourself the questions below. If you answer "Yes" to at least one of the questions, then there is room for that item on your to-do list. If not, add it to your to-don't list.

○ *Does this support one of my RBGs?*

○ *Is this a fundamental part of my job description?*

○ *Is this work visible and/or does it give me access to a valuable connection?*

○ *Does this work bring me joy, and do I want to continue to make time for it?*

Download a digital postcard version of these questions that's perfect for pinning on your bulletin board or saving on your phone. Scan the QR code or go to franhauser.com/loveyourcareer.

Now, I wish you could just add stuff to your to-don't list and—poof!—find it's gone. Some things you might be able to just stop doing. Others may require buy-in from your manager or delegation to someone else. In the second column on your to-don't list, add the first thing you need to do to get this off your plate (e.g., for Maria, her first step was to call the head of the school task force).

Your To-Don't List

Task/Project	Next Step

I hope that looking at this list is freeing. I know it was for me the first time I put one together. Now, to actually get work-related stuff off your list, have a conversation with your manager and use your RBGs as justification for the reprioritization. During your next meeting, say something like, "I really want to make sure I'm making the best use of my time, and I realized that I was devoting too much time to X, Y, and Z but that they're not adding value to the company. I wanted to let you know that I'm planning on deprioritizing those things unless you think they're adding more value than I realize."

Distractors and fillers

A calendar and to-do list assessment won't reveal everything on your mental load. It would take you hours to calculate all the invisible tasks that take up precious time and space, and it's very easy to fill our days with what I call distractors and fillers. These extraneous tasks and roles—like agreeing to take notes in a meeting, planning the next happy hour, and being the person who always trains new employees—aren't always value creators and are, simply put, time sucks. The nuance here is that being helpful and going out of your way for others does help you build relationships vital to career growth *and* being a giver, doer, and nurturer are strong qualities and characteristics of leadership and success. To be mindful about the choices you make and the time you allot for work, ask yourself the same check-in questions as you evaluate potential distractors and fillers:

○ *Does this support one of my RBGs?*

○ *Is this a fundamental part of my job description?*

○ *Is this work visible and/or does it give me access to a valuable connection?*

○ *Does this work bring me joy, and do I want to continue to make time for it?*

Distractors: These are tasks indirectly related to your work that prevent you from focusing on your priorities. Distractors at work are inevitable, but women are often loaded with the additional roles of emotional therapist, culture builder, and conflict resolver. Distractor tasks tend to revolve around people and culture; consider examples such as getting stuck in never-ending conversations with colleagues or organizing a team celebration because no one else will do it. In a silo, these tasks can serve an important purpose in helping people feel connected, but they become a problem when they take over your to-do list.

Distractors to your already maxed-out job can distract *you* from investing in your own career.

Can you think of common distractors that show up at work for you? Use this space to brainstorm and then, if they're not already there, transfer them over to your to-don't list (where they belong!).

Fillers: These are tasks that are directly related to work but are often extraneous and "fill" your time with to-dos that are not highly valued. Studies show that women tend to take on (or are asked to take on) more of these filler tasks, such as scheduling meetings and ordering lunch or being the memory keeper, the organizer, the person who keeps the trains on the track but goes unnoticed.

Can you think of common fillers that show up at work for you? Use this space to brainstorm and then, if they're not already there, transfer these tasks over to your to-don't list (where they belong!).

....

....

....

....

....

....

Next, you will learn how to say "No" to things like this, so they never make it onto your to-do list in the first place.

2

SAY "NO"

The case for saying "No"

Simply put, saying "No" frees you up to work on the things that matter . . . the things that are going to drive success for your company *and* for your own personal and professional development.

How many times have you found yourself in a position where you wish you could go back in time and say "No"? NO to joining a useless committee, NO to doing a favor where you feel taken advantage of, NO to the tenth networking event this month. When you say "Yes" ALL THE TIME, your sense of self diminishes and your clarity becomes clouded. When you are doing everything, you start to lose sight of your goals, your unique values, and what brings you joy. In the end, this affects your confidence and the way others perceive you.

It's hard to say "No"

Saying "No" at work didn't come easy to me, especially earlier on in my career. I was just a few weeks into my maternity leave after adopting my second son when I heard that the company had named a new CEO. Immediately colleagues emailed me, urging me to come back and start making a good impression. Anxiety set in. As any mother knows, maternity leave is a complicated time: The fear of being forgotten or being "found out" that you're not essential is real; you fear that you're missing out on important decisions being made.

I felt vulnerable and worried that if I didn't return I would be seen as uncommitted or, worse, obsolete. So I cut my maternity leave short and went back to work. In retrospect, I could have reached out to the CEO and asked to meet for lunch to make a connection and then continued my leave. Instead, I allowed my aversion to saying "No" to take over my decision, and my boundaries came crashing down.

I know I'm not the only one who has fallen into this trap. I sent out a quick survey to three hundred professional women in my network to probe deeper and ask, *Why are we taking all of it on? Why are we not saying "No"?* The response was overwhelming—seventy-five women answered within two hours. These weren't quick thoughts—it became a venting session. Women revealed that they feel a constant need to prove themselves; they said they don't have the respect, authority, and job security to say "No," so they say "Yes." But a lot of the responses also uncovered deep ties to one's self-worth and to finding satisfaction in being asked to do something.

What's holding you back from saying "No"?

"Awareness is a powerful catalyst for positive change," writes personal coach and author Cheryl Richardson, so let's gain awareness. Consider this: Why do you have a hard time saying "No"? Is it due to people pleasing, fear of missing out (FOMO), a desire to be in control, or something else? The reasons survey respondents gave for saying "Yes" when they should have said "I wish I could . . ." were many.

Among those reasons, they:

- worried about not being valued at work in the broader sense
- were inclined to be a people pleaser
- wanted to be seen as a team player
- were afraid to relinquish control
- felt validated when needed, with many women equating their worth with their work
- felt vulnerable in their role after having children
- felt it was a side cost of being the only woman with a seat at the table
- had "FOMO" or fear of being left out of the information flow
- felt bound by a superhero complex, or not wanting to give the impression that they can't handle it all
- felt they needed to be perfect at all times
- had a fear of failure

✏️ **When you read the list above, which ones did you have visceral reactions to? Highlight or circle those entries or write your own here (it can be more than one).**

If you're still feeling as if you can't or don't want to say "No," check in with yourself using the awareness work above. Are you saying "Yes" for the right reason? If people pleasing struck a chord with you, recognizing and being aware that this is the reason why you have a hard time saying "No" can empower you to set better boundaries. When a request comes in, ask yourself, "Am I saying 'Yes' because I am in people-pleasing mode?"

Press "pause"

When you're in the moment of making a decision, there is often a knee-jerk reaction to say "Yes" because it's easier than saying "No." In the long run, this is unsustainable, and you've created more work for yourself that may not be aligned with your RBGs. That's why you need to press "pause" when you receive a request in your inbox or in person. Ask yourself the same check-in questions from the prior exercise so you can be intentional about your response:

○ *Does this support one of my RBGs?*

○ *Is this a fundamental part of my job description?*

○ *Is this work visible and/or does it give me access to a valuable connection?*

○ *Does this work bring me joy, and do I want to continue to make time for it?*

Tip: Enlist your manager to help you say "No."

Even when it's a last-minute request from a client or one directly from your boss, you still need to be intentional about your workload. Ask your manager to help you prioritize and decide whether it's worth your time. You can say, "Yes, I can do that, but I will have to stop doing X or it will take the place of Y. Are you okay with that?" You will feel more empowered to push back when you bring them into the decision-making process.

Favor: To Do or Not to Do?

Early in my career, I always said "Yes" whenever someone more senior asked me for a favor, knowing that this person was good to have on my side. Picking up coffee, taking notes, making lunch reservations—sure, why not? I was happy to do favors or errands for others when I had an authentic desire to do so or a strategic reason for doing it, such as gaining an invite to a key meeting. But eventually, these strategic lines became blurry, and I knew I required a boundary. I came up with what I call the "Rule of Three." If someone had asked me for the same "favor" more than three times in a span of thirty days, I knew that I was no longer "helping," but, rather, that my colleague had developed—and I had encouraged—a bad habit.

Here is one of my favorite time-saving tips: Find the sweet spot between "Yes" and "No." Requests for your time, energy, or expertise often seem like "Yes" or "No" propositions, but there is actually plenty of space to be helpful in between. When there is a strategic reason for you to be helpful, or when you really care about the person asking for help, you need to find a gray zone that allows you to deliver assistance in a way that protects your workflow. Here's what you can say: "I can't do that now, but here's what I can do . . ." Then, suggest a lower-lift way to assist, such as brainstorming instead of execution. Can you offer to attend part of a meeting or event or to proofread something instead of doing a full edit? These part-dos are the sweet spot where you can add value without taking on the full responsibility, and you can still be giving while protecting your time and boundaries.

Here are some examples to get your juices flowing:

I can't do that . . .	. . . but I can do this
Attend the event	Promote it on social media
Participate on that committee	Make an introduction to someone who potentially can
Take the lead on running a project or event	Help brainstorm some ideas
Attend the entire meeting	Pop in at the end to hear the wrap-up
Go out for a "pick my brain" coffee	Have a fifteen-minute office hours session

To say "No" with kindness, decline with confidence. Start with "Thank you" instead of "I'm sorry." You don't need to apologize for turning down a request. Say, "Thank you for the opportunity" or "Thank you for thinking of me," and then add that you're at full capacity right now. If this is a close relationship, you may want to be specific about why you can't do it: "I'm focusing on x, y, or z." If it's not a close relationship, it's fine to simply say that you wish you could help, but your plate is full. If you're feeling generous, you can always offer a different time line ("I will be free in July") or a smaller assist, such as suggesting someone else who would be up for the task or sharing research on a smaller piece that needs to be done. This keeps you focused on your RBGs while still coming across as a team player. Whatever you decide, be clear. And wrap it up with a positive sentiment.

🖉 **Write out your "kind 'No'" in two sentences. (No need to overexplain—keep it short and sweet.)**

You may want to create a canned email response that you have easy access to!

How to Say "No" Kindly

If the answer is a "No," I want to share with you a few easy steps to create a kind way to say it.

1	Thank you
2	My plate is full
3	Say "No" (or offer a lower-lift way to assist)
4	Best wishes

"I'M ACTUALLY AS PROUD OF THE THINGS WE *haven't done* AS THE THINGS WE HAVE DONE."

—Steve Jobs

3

CHANGE THE WAY YOU WORK

Going back to when I returned from maternity leave, I had a huge realization that if I wanted to create clear boundaries and spend quality time with my family I would need to change the way that I worked. There were a few key insights that I had:

- Lose the FOMO.
- Share the "Yes."
- Say "No" to perfection.
- Multitasking doesn't work.

Lose the FOMO

There are times in my career when I had major FOMO and didn't want to miss out. To create more time and space, I had to become choosier when it came to invitations to join workplace committees, brainstorming meetings, or networking events. I started to evaluate whether something was a real career growth opportunity, and whether this was an experience that would be reciprocal and energizing or I would just come back from the event feeling depleted.

Use these questions:

- ***Optional Meetings:*** *Does this meeting give you a seat at the table where an important decision is being made, or will it give you access to knowledge or an opportunity to share your voice? Will it be a résumé or visibility builder? Does your boss care about this topic?*

○ **Networking Events:** *Is there someone attending who can help you with one of your RBGs, or is there a skill or knowledge being shared that will have an impact on how you do your job?*

○ **Committees/Side Projects:** *Is there someone on the committee you're trying to get access to? Is this an opportunity to help build a better, more inclusive culture at work?*

If you can't answer "Yes" to any of these questions, the particular invitation you're evaluating is probably not worth your time. Visibility doesn't equate to value if it's preventing you from doing important things on your list. Get creative on how you can get what you need without being there in person. For example, ask for a meeting recap from someone who was there and/or follow up with an idea via email to your manager or another senior person in the meeting.

Find the JOMO

JOMO is the opposite of FOMO—it's the JOY of missing out. Review your calendar for the last few months and think about any optional meetings/events that you attended that, in hindsight, were not a good use of your time. What could you have done instead that would have been more impactful?

🖊 ***Brainstorm what you would do with "found" time, from skipping a meeting or passing on a project. Use this as a reminder when you are thinking about saying "Yes" in the future!***

Share the "Yes"

You will still get credit when you delegate thoughtfully.

One woman I know, Lisa, who works at a major tech company, was "volun-told" (her word, which I love) to plan an offsite for 1,500 people. She was frustrated but ready to do it all on her own. I suggested she needed to get a team of people in place and begin delegating ASAP. If she spent her valuable time as a leader instead of a sole executor, it would help support her RBG of becoming a manager. I told Lisa: "The best leaders know how to motivate and rally a team to get it all done. Set up a Slack channel; ask for help." Getting the same work done thoughtfully, instead of stuffing goodie bags at 1 a.m., would showcase Lisa as "leadership material" and set her up for a promotion into a management role.

Who can lighten your load?

There is an art to delegation. Delegation is not simply passing a project off to someone else; it's getting them excited about the opportunity. We all have people in our lives who we can lean on to lighten our loads; we also all know people who are looking for a chance to prove their own value.

Make a list of the people in your life who could benefit from extra responsibility. If resources are stretched thin across your organization, look outside your work circle to, say, college students you're mentoring or people you do volunteer work with. Where are they looking to grow? Do you see any natural overlaps?

Say "No" to perfection

Being imperfect allows you to make time for the things that matter.

Recently I served as a mentor for a start-up accelerator program. To the founders, I was like *Project Runway*'s Tim Gunn, but for me it was an early look at a number of impressive companies that would allow me to put capital to work. I sat through many meetings with each of the groups and left them with action items to follow up on. Without fail, the male founders quickly did what I advised and sent their pitches back to me, with (minor) typos and all. We had multiple meetings to continue the work on their decks. Meanwhile, the female founders took two or three weeks to perfect their presentations, and by that time the momentum was gone. They were so worried about making everything beautiful and perfect that they missed out on vital mentoring time and professional opportunities.

I've personally experienced this kind of obsession with perfection. How many times did I create a PowerPoint deck versus just simply having a conversation with my boss about a new idea or opportunity? How often did I spend crazy amounts of hours perfecting a report that was only being used for internal purposes, making it beautiful versus making sure the content was meaningful? These habits rose to the surface after I returned from maternity leave. I realized that I could save so much time by changing the way that I approached these types of work interactions.

Perfection is overrated and can often jeopardize your growth. The invisible pressure women put on themselves to make sure they can do everything well—better than well or *perfect*—is contributing to career cost opportunity.

What's your MVP?

Minimum viable product, or MVP, is a technology concept that I think is beneficial for everyone. The idea is that you launch your product with just enough features to be usable for early customers who can provide feedback. It's a first draft, in essence. Embracing this way of working will make you the real MVP—in this case, the most valuable player. If perfection is something that seeps into your work life, think about a task or project where, in hindsight, you now realize you spent an inordinate amount of time perfecting it. What would have been the impact on the task if you had spent less time fixated on it? Would the quality have suffered in a material way? Or would the result have been "good enough"?

Write your reflections here.

Part of the perfection trap is becoming comfortable with showing early work. It takes confidence to realize that your credibility and worth should not be tied to a first draft. To find that confidence, assemble your own antiperfection team. Who do you trust to be one of your "early customers" or reviewers? Who can you be vulnerable with?

 **Write down their names and make a plan to ask them to help you with this goal.**

Multitasking doesn't work

The majority of people cannot multitask effectively. Only 2.5 percent of all people can effectively switch back and forth between complex activities. This has to do with the way the human brain is wired. Instead, as best as you can, try to schedule your time in chunks: creative writing for X hours, a specific project for Y hours, and so on. Group things together that make sense to be together. This is especially true for your inbox. I am so much more productive when I address all emails related to a specific project, instead of addressing them chronologically. (You can search by sender or topic to sort.) It's my version of the Pomodoro method, which encourages you to get in the zone for one specific task or project for twenty-five minutes. Focusing on one to-do or group of to-dos helps you get through your work much more quickly than switching from topic to topic. When I embarked on writing this book, I decided to get up earlier and start writing by 6:00 a.m. It gave me two undistracted hours (before the kids get up) when my brain is at its most fresh to be productive, versus fitting in bits of time throughout the day.

When are you most likely to multitask? Choose a random day and make notes of the moments you find yourself trying to multitask. Is it when you're on a project you don't like? When you have to be creative? A certain time of day? Is there a pattern or common trigger? Use this space to write down your observations.

Once you're aware of the patterns or triggers, you can be more proactive. Turn off notifications on your laptop and phone during the times when you're feeling the need to break your focus.

Time Killers

Time Builders

○ Useless meetings ·······> Get the recap

○ PowerPoint deck ·······> Conversation

○ Obsessing over form ·······> Focus on content

○ Perfection ·······> Good enough

○ Multitasking ·······> Time blocking

○ Taking it all on ·······> Share the "Yes"

✎ **Add yours!**

·······>

·······>

·······>

·······>

·······>

·······>

·······>

Pause and Reflect

Distractions are everywhere. It's nearly impossible to focus on work and your goals when you don't feel in control of your time and what's on your to-do list. That's why it's so crucial to learn how to set boundaries at work, cut out extraneous tasks, and prioritize your own needs so you can focus on the things that matter most to you and your career. When you give yourself permission to say "No" or to finish up a project when it's "good enough," you will feel more focused and less frenzied. In the end, you'll create the time and space you need to achieve your RBGs. Next, it's time to tackle the inner work that will allow you to own your strengths and leave you feeling more self-assured than ever!

Meditation

Find a comfortable place for this reflection. Begin by focusing on your breath to find stillness.

When we prioritize our own needs, we're actually better able to serve others.

Think of a time when you said "Yes," but what you really wanted to say was "No." This may have been at work or at home. It may have been professional or personal.

How did that decision impact your energy, your mood, your attitude, and ultimately your perspective? Becoming more aware of how you feel can empower you to make better choices. Setting and honoring boundaries takes practice, but when you make choices that are in alignment with your goals and values, you feel the difference. It's worth it.

The dance between "Yes" and "No" is easier to understand when we realize the impact our decisions have on us. Setting clear boundaries with kindness can make a profound difference on how we feel.

And, rather than saying "No," you might have an opportunity to say "Yes" in a different way. The sense of freedom you will feel when you make decisions that are aligned with your purpose and goals can be life changing.

 If you would prefer to listen to the meditation, scan the QR code or visit franhauser.com/loveyourcareer.

Musings, Downloads, and Doodles

Know Your Value

I find that when I know my value, when I feel good about who I am and am clear about what I am setting out to do, nothing can stop me. Section 3 helped you create time and space to work on your RBGs; section 4 is focused on leaning into your strengths so that you can approach your work with self-assurance.

Self-assurance grows when you have a deep sense of WHO you are (your traits and abilities) and start to pay close attention to WHAT you've accomplished and what has worked for you. It grows when you understand the obstacles in front of you—even the self-imposed ones—and how to prevent them from blocking you. When you're self-assured and can recognize your value, work feels more effortless and enjoyable. Doesn't that sound good?

self-assurance:

CONFIDENCE IN ONE'S OWN ABILITIES OR CHARACTER.

You Are Awesome. Let's Start There

Everyone has superpowers. Superpowers can come in the form of character traits (like being kind and doing the right thing) or talents (like being able to diffuse a situation or being great with numbers). These are the things that make you YOU and help you stand out from the crowd. Think about the traits and talents that make you awesome. There is space over the next few pages for you to write them down.

If you're stuck, ask your colleagues and friends to describe your character in a few words and to name three strengths or ways that you shine at work. I know it may feel awkward, but tell them you're doing an activity to help clarify and reach your career goals and you would appreciate their help on this next step. Add the compliments and affirmations they send back on these pages, too.

YOUR SUPERPOWERS

🖉 *Character Traits:*

_____

_____

_____

_____

🖉 *Talents:*

_____

_____

_____

_____

🖉 *Add the superpowers that mean the most to you on the next page. You can draw them or create a word cloud, whatever makes you happiest. Snap a pic so that you have this available at your fingertips.*

These are the qualities that make you YOU and enable you to create value. If you ever need a pick-me-up, come back to these words.

MATCH YOUR SUPERPOWERS TO YOUR RBGS

Let's go a little deeper. When you look at each word, can you think of an example where the quality (whether it's a character trait or strength) served you (and your career) well? These foundational strengths are the secret sauce to achieving your RBGs. For example, if one of your strengths is that you are great at helping people come together and see each other's perspective, you can speak to this quality when pitching yourself to be on a cross-departmental project that will require many different teams to work together.

🖊 *Writing down your superpowers here will serve as a reminder that you have what it takes to realize your RBGs.*

RBG	Supporting Superpowers

EMBRACE YOUR TOO

Sometimes superpowers can be misinterpreted by others. Have you ever been told that you're *TOO* forgiving, too aggressive, too quiet, too flashy, too [fill in the blank]? I can't even count how many times I have been told that I'm TOO nice. My voice coaches at Vital Voice Training have said to embrace your TOO because it can be one of your greatest sources of strength. I love this message and wholeheartedly agree—it was part of the inspiration for my book *The Myth of the Nice Girl.* In that book, I wrote about how being nice has been a strength for me throughout my career because when you're (authentically) nice to people, they trust you, and relationships are built on trust. I was able to build relationships with colleagues who helped me gain access to resources (both money and employees), championed me for promotions, and helped me get buy-in from management.

Finding your authenticity and being genuine is about being your true self at work, whether that's about niceness or another superpower. I know it's not always easy, especially when faced with a workplace culture that penalizes you if you don't fit a company's mold. If and when that's the case, flex your authenticity muscles little by little, and you just may empower others around you to do the same.

✎ What is your TOO? What have managers or colleagues said about you in a review or through feedback? Write it down here. How can you articulate it as a strength?

(Example: Too stubborn > Stick up for what you believe.)

Redefine Failure and Fear

When I was at AOL (back in the dot-com days!), I was asked to pull together a strategy presentation for a few of our brands. I was given one month to do it. I had recently started working for a new manager, and I was eager to impress. I worked really hard on it. When the time came to make the presentation, I presented it not only to my manager but also to a group of colleagues. Let's just say that the presentation didn't go anywhere near as well as I had hoped. My manager used words like "You missed the boat on what I was looking for." Yikes.

If YOU TAKE A RISK AND IT DOESN'T GO AS PLANNED, *welcome to the club.*

In this situation, what didn't go well is pretty obvious: I under-delivered on the strategy presentation. My learning takeaway was that given that I had an entire month to complete the project (with very little direction), it would have been helpful to have checked in with my manager to make sure I was on the right track and meeting her expectations. The bigger takeaway for me was the realization that my approach to any responsibility included the idea that I never wanted to be a burden; I wanted to show that I was able to figure it out all on my own. It took this experience for me to realize how flawed this thinking is, and I used this learning moment to inform the way that I worked going forward.

Self-assurance is cumulative; it's based on both positive and negative situations. I like to think of failure as success-in-training. A setback can become a launchpad when you look at it as an opportunity for growth and development. In the end, what we show and tell ourselves is the most powerful tool we have to finding true self-assurance.

On the next page, write down a few things from the past year (or so) that didn't quite go as planned. Or revisit your formal review and reflect on the feedback you've received. Think about what you learned from the experiences, but, even more important, think about how these relate to your RBGs. What can you learn from them going forward? Are there specific skill gaps that stand out? What is worth an investment in time to learn? For example, if you received poor feedback on a speech you gave and building industry visibility is important to you, can you reach out to a colleague who is known for public speaking? Look into a course? Make a list here.

What Didn't Go Well	Learning Takeaway

TURN YOUR THOUGHTS AROUND

I find that when self-doubt, imposter syndrome, or career envy takes over, it's nearly impossible to stay focused on my goals. Does this happen to you, too? One trick I like to use is reframing negative thinking. It's a glass half-full approach where you flip the script of your internal narrative. For instance, if you were invited to a meeting with all the highest level execs, your natural inclination might be to think, "I'm going to be surrounded by all these brilliant people, and they're going to figure me out." Instead, write down, "There is a reason I was invited. I belong here. I'm going to be surrounded by all these brilliant people, and I will learn so much!" Research shows that by reframing the thought in a positive way, your brain and body will begin to believe it.

Write down some common imposter thoughts that you experience. Then write the opposite way to look at the same scenario.

Imposter Thought	Positive Spin

Self-assurance

IS A SKILL YOU DEVELOP BY PAYING CLOSE ATTENTION TO YOUR SUCCESSES IN LIFE AND

how

YOU ACCOMPLISHED THEM.

Self-Assurance: Facts Versus Fiction

If you struggle with feeling self-assured, you're not alone. We all feel like that sometimes.

To this day, when I'm struggling with a decision or feeling insecure, I go back to the evidence. It's really hard to argue with facts. I think about what I have done that's worked, how I did it, and what the outcome was. When I was at Time Inc., I was asked to give a speech to three hundred managers, and I was nervous. A close friend told me, "Think back and remember a time when you gave a good speech." It was simple but solid advice. Before delivering that big presentation, I thought back to a speech I'd given a few years before that my team said really resonated with them. I visualized that speech in as much detail as I could possibly remember: what I'd said, how I'd said it, and how it had felt to succeed. This made me feel far more confident.

This purposeful self-reflection will result in what I call evidence-based confidence. To develop your own, start keeping a list of your successes to look back on whenever those feelings of self-doubt creep up. Also include any insights you gained around the process to achieve that successful outcome. Self-assurance builds not just from wins but also from the confidence that comes with repeatable actions. For me, when I figured out the best way to prepare for a speech, I felt more in control before the next one because I could rely on a process that worked for me in the past.

Smile File

I keep my successes, affirmations, and accolades in a journal. Allow this workbook to be your journal. I've created space here for you to start your list and add to it. I started calling it my Smile File after I heard a colleague use that phrase when referring to a folder in her inbox where she saves positive, affirming emails. (I love this idea, too!)

On the following pages, write down positive feedback or insight you've received, when it was said, and who said it. It can even be from the distant past—praise is not perishable! You could copy and tape smile-worthy emails here, too; use this as your success scrapbook.

When you are in those moments of doubt, look at this list and remind yourself of the great work you've done and how much value you have created already. Think about specific details and how you felt during those successes.

Smile File

Smile File

Smile File

Smile File

THE "CONFIDENCE GAP"

Your Smile File is a powerful asset against self-doubt. Sadly, I've seen that many of the women I've worked with and mentored over the years are less likely to truly believe in their capabilities than their male peers. When Hewlett-Packard was looking to place more women in top leadership positions, they found that women were likely to apply for a job only when they believed they met a full 100 percent of the qualifications listed for the job. In other words, they applied only if they were a perfect match for the role. Men, on the other hand, applied if they met only 60 percent of the qualifications. That's the confidence gap.

I admit I've been guilty of this at times in my own career. I was working at AOL when I heard that senior leadership was putting together a team to bridge the gap between AOL and Time, Inc. (both divisions of Time Warner). This opportunity sounded like a great fit for me, and I loved the idea of working on the Time, Inc. brands like *Fortune*, *PEOPLE*, and *InStyle*. I wanted to step up, but I was intimidated. I had never worked in magazine publishing, and I found myself second-guessing my own qualifications.

I had a male colleague at AOL who had the same level of experience as me, but unlike me, he jumped to make this move right away. Knowing that I had strong interpersonal skills, he encouraged me to join him. As it turned out, taking that opportunity led me to a whole new career at Time, Inc.

I now know that my colleague and I unwittingly exemplified the most common behaviors of our genders; it's typical for men to step up right away, while equally qualified women tend to hang back and wait to be pulled in. So, if women are losing ground because we undervalue ourselves, what can we do about it? The first step, as simple as it may sound, is to be aware. If an opportunity comes your way that intrigues you but you think you may not be qualified for it, remind yourself that you probably are a better fit than you realize.

Then adjust your self-assessment. Remember the study showing that men often apply for jobs when they meet only 60 percent of the qualifications. So ask yourself, "Am I 60 percent qualified for this opportunity?" If the answer is "Yes," go for it. A man with the exact same qualifications as you probably would.

"Am I 60 percent qualified for this opportunity?" If the answer is "Yes," go for it.

Pause and Reflect

Check in with yourself: How's your mood? Your mindset? Do you feel confident and capable to embrace the work and love your career? I hope so! When you're having a down moment or a setback and need a confidence boost, revisit this section. Self-assurance can have a profound impact on your life—on the choices you make, on the way you react to difficult situations, and on your ability to invest in your career by doing the hard work every day. You and your mindset will help lead you to success, but, I've learned, having a support system can make the journey even more effective and fun. That's up next.

Meditation

Noticing your breath, take a moment to be still. When we're quiet and still, we can sink below the chatter of the mind. Grounded in this stillness, it is easier to feel self-assured and recognize our value.

Often the stories we tell ourselves are just that . . . stories. They are not the truth. When your mind is telling you a story that you're not good enough, go back to the facts. Reflect on an experience at work where you created real value or a moment where you used your superpowers for good. Know that you are able to shape and change the conversation in your head. Know that your thoughts are not always reality.

When you are confident in your character and in your own abilities, you are more comfortable in your own skin. You bring beauty, lightness, and joy into the world. When this is overshadowed by self-doubt, the positive impact that you're having on others can also be overshadowed.

If you are feeling self-doubt, continue to look within yourself. Find a sense of comfort in how far you've come in your journey so far. Take small steps. Open yourself up to the possibilities that lie before you. You have all the power you need within you.

Self-assurance is a deeply rooted faith in yourself; it's a sense of being grounded in who you truly are. As you move on with your day, remember to stay connected to what is within you.

Believe in yourself.

 If you would prefer to listen to the meditation, scan the QR code or visit franhauser.com/loveyourcareer.

Musings, Downloads, and Doodles

Build Your Dream Team

You don't have to go through this career journey alone. In fact, when you *don't* go through it alone, you multiply your chance for success. That's what the best start-up founders do. I spend a lot of time with entrepreneurs, investing in their businesses and advising them, and I often coach them on the importance of building a strategic board of advisors who are experienced, have access to important networks, and foster learning opportunities.

I believe you should treat your career the same way that founders treat their businesses! You, too, can assemble a dream team that supports you and helps you reach your RBGs. It can be a combination of people you already know, who have always been encouraging you, and new relationships you develop along the way. By the end of this section, you will have identified a few key people who will be there to guide you and inspire you.

Create Your Dream Team

The first person who took an interest in my career path was my boss Lou, at Ernst & Young. He's the one who told me that I needed to voice my opinions in meetings instead of just saying, "That's interesting!" He saw my strengths and helped me play to them while also filling in the gaps in my knowledge and experience. Overall, this relationship gave me a tremendous amount of confidence and know-how early on in my career. Lou was the very first member of my dream team.

Your dream team is like having your own personal board of advisors. Your advisors shouldn't just be cheerleaders who hype you up (though that's nice every once in a while). These are people who can counsel you when you have an important career decision to make, help boost your confidence when you're feeling as if you don't belong, and provide introductions for you with people who can be helpful.

As you're assembling your dream team, think about how much there is to learn from people who are different from you. Whether that difference is of race, gender, sexual orientation, faith, socioeconomic status, there is so much to gain from people with different world perspectives. Don't create an echo chamber (a dream team that looks and sounds like you). In fact, as you're thinking about the connections you want to make, put yourself in rooms that are outside your current career track to expose yourself to new points of view.

WHERE DO YOU NEED SUPPORT?

When great leaders assemble a team, they think about what's missing. Maybe it's someone who is super analytical, who can bring a global perspective, or who has become an expert in a specific coding language. I believe it's always best to hire someone who can help fill your gaps and who you can learn from. That's what your dream team can do for you.

Look back at your Career Action Plan on page 64 and write down all four of your RBGs here. Then think about what kind of support you need to reach each RBG. It could be specific knowledge (how to integrate a new technology platform, for example) or exposure to senior leaders at work. What kind of advisors would be most helpful as you begin to build your dream team?

RBG	Support Needed

DRAFT YOUR TEAM

This is a sample of the types of people who are beneficial to have in your support system. Feel free to make it your own!

Dream team member 1:
An internal champion

If you're currently in a job, think of people at your company whose leadership style you like and who have influence. Don't focus just on senior management. There may be an informal power network to consider as well—people who have access to knowledge and resources. These are people who can champion you when there is a new role opening up at the company or help you navigate tricky situations.

Brainstorm a list of potential candidates. You can keep coming back to this list as you interact with different people at work.

Dream team member 2:
A confidant who keeps you in check

This is someone in your personal life who knows your values intimately. This is critical. Whether it's a family member or a close friend, this is someone who can be there for you when you're feeling frustrated and need to vent or you need help making an important decision. You may already know who this person is for you. Lean on them. When I get into a situation at work where things start turning emotional, I often stop and say, "Let's regroup on this tomorrow." Pausing and stepping away allows you to respond thoughtfully versus react emotionally. I usually find that after I go home and vent to my husband or my sister (and get a good night's sleep), I'm ready to have a more productive conversation. Having a sounding board and not being afraid to be vulnerable and ask for help will create headspace—just by simply getting the words out of your mind and into the world.

Dream team member 3:
A mentor or a coach

This is someone who is really good at mentoring/coaching. This member is especially important if the person you selected in #1 makes for a great champion but not a great mentor. There is a difference. A champion will make sure you get considered when a new role opens up at the company, but they may not have the bandwidth or interest to teach/coach. When you think about potential mentors, the sweet spot is finding someone who can open doors for you AND will spend the time with you when you need it. If you're having a tough time coming up with people, write down the type of mentoring/coaching you're looking for. The next time you're meeting with your manager or a colleague you have a close relationship with, discuss this with them. They might have great ideas for you and may be able to make introductions.

Dream team member 4:
A supportive peer

This is someone who you can learn from (maybe they have different skills, backgrounds, or experiences). Some of my best mentors have been peers; whether it was during my time at Coke or *PEOPLE* magazine, they were the ones who pushed me to go for the job I didn't think I was ready for. They backed me up when I was presenting an unconventional idea and helped me when I needed fresh eyes on something. There's also a level of comfort and safety—with peer mentors you can be less filtered than you may be with senior leaders. Don't underestimate the power of camaraderie and feeling that you have your tribe who is there for you.

Dream team member 5:
A leader you admire

This is someone who you see as a future you—maybe they are working in an industry you'd like to break into or maybe you love their leadership style and want to learn from them. Don't assume that anyone is out of reach. This is not a place for negative thinking like "That person would never take a meeting with me." Keep yourself open to the possibility. Also include people you'd like to reconnect with (especially those who've had a big impact on you and your career).

YOUR DREAM TEAM

You may already have people on your dream team. Include them here. Add others as you build those relationships. And, of course, add more circles if you need to! Your dream team will flow and grow over time.

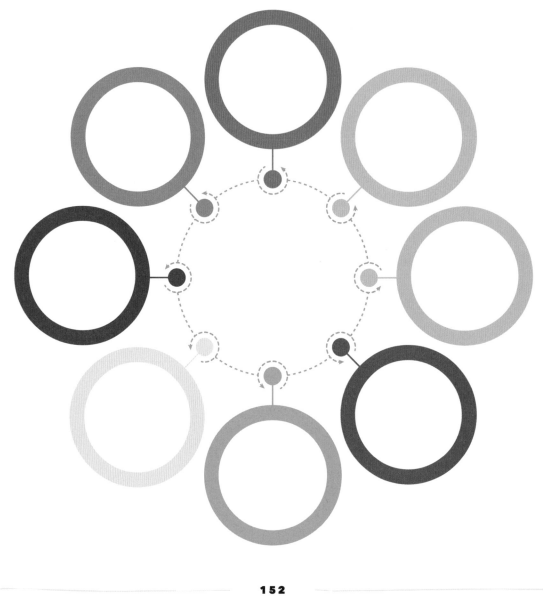

Your
———
DREAM TEAM
———
WILL GROUND YOU
WHEN YOU'RE LOST AND
inspire you
WHEN YOU'RE STUCK.

How to Reach Out Successfully

So now that you have an idea of who you'd like to be on your dream team, how do you actually make it happen? And, what do you do if you don't already have a relationship with someone you'd like to have on the team?

I've found that the most effective way to do outreach is through a warm introduction. LinkedIn is great for researching mutual connections. Also, writing a short email that your mutual colleague or friend can forward makes it easy to make the warm introduction.

If you do need to reach out cold, don't just ask, offer. A young woman messaged me on LinkedIn to ask for advice. A regular occurrence, right? But this woman also offered to share some social media ideas for the start-ups that I advise (she had researched my portfolio). This caught my attention. If you are reaching out cold, express how you can be helpful. It would have been difficult for me to justify taking that meeting given the demands on my time, but she made it easy for me to say "Yes."

Don't underestimate the value that you can bring to someone who is more "senior" to you. I did a virtual talk for the "Women in Sales" class at the University of Cincinnati. At the end of my presentation, the professor asked me what the students can do to be helpful. I was actually in the process of writing this book, so I responded that I could use some beta readers and would love their help promoting the book on social media. One of the students followed up with me on email asking if I would be open to doing a brief chat with her, and in return she offered to give me some ideas for how to promote the book to college students. Win-win!

I find it's so helpful to have go-to phrases when sending that initial invite:

- ○ *I'm such a fan of yours . . .*
- ○ *I noticed that you're doing . . .*
- ○ *Your career journey is so impressive . . .*

Do any of these resonate with you?

✐ **Use this space to capture a few more ideas.**

TIP SHEET: BEFORE, DURING, AND AFTER THE FIRST MEETING

1. **Do your homework.** Come to the meeting prepared with specific questions about the person's career, company, projects, or passions. Don't stick with small talk about the person's career trajectory. That can be an instant turn-off.

2. **Be action-oriented and grateful.** Two questions you should ask at the end of every meeting: "Is there anyone you think I should meet?" and "How can I be helpful to you?"

3. **Send a thank-you note.** Always.

4. **Nurture the connection.** Send a note with follow-ups and updates on how you've acted on their advice or introduction. Send links to articles you think they might find interesting. Congratulate them when they get a promotion. Do whatever feels authentic for you but keep that relationship warm.

5. **Don't force a relationship.** Both sides have to feel it. You know when you leave a first meeting with someone and you have an awesome feeling . . . you're energized, and you want to see them again. That applies here. The best relationships develop organically.

CONNECTING FOR INTROVERTS

Those who have a harder time putting themselves out there may be having heart palpitations right now. You're not alone. You'd be surprised how many confident, intelligent women hold themselves back by not speaking up in front of others, not reaching out to potential contacts, or not introducing themselves at important meetings or events. I'm always surprised to see this, BUT I also understand it. I've been there myself.

Very early on in my career, when I was assigned to pretty big projects, I found myself in face-to-face meetings with high-powered executives. There was one executive in particular who I found to be so intimidating. I was nervous to speak when he was in the room, so I didn't. I know what it feels like to have something you really, really want to say, and it's right at the tip of your tongue, and then you hold back. I realized that all I needed was a way to insert myself into the conversation. I often use the following phrases to do just that:

- *Building on that . . .*
- *I wonder if we flipped that idea on its head . . .*
- *Following on that . . .*
- *I love that perspective and . . .*

If you have difficulty reaching out or speaking up, think about what fears or stories are getting in your way. Are you afraid to reach out because you fear you might be judged or that you won't know what to say? Can you identify the fear that might be preventing you from sending that email?

Take some time to write some reflections here. As you begin to let go of that fear, your self-assurance will shine through.

Also, think about the worst-case scenario: What happens if they say "No," don't respond, or ghost you? You move on. Remember this one simple idea: The next time you're agonizing over extending an invitation or inserting yourself into a conversation, stop and ask yourself: Why not?

MEET THEM WHERE THEY ARE (LITERALLY)

Connections that you make serendipitously can also be amazing. I've met so many incredible people at conferences, industry events, or on social media platforms like Instagram and LinkedIn. Where do people that inspire you hang out? Go THERE. And remind yourself that most people who are at these types of events or on social media are also looking to make connections. They want to meet interesting people and continue to learn and grow themselves.

Can you think of one conference/event to attend or a social media platform where you can more actively engage? If you're not sure, ask other members of your dream team!

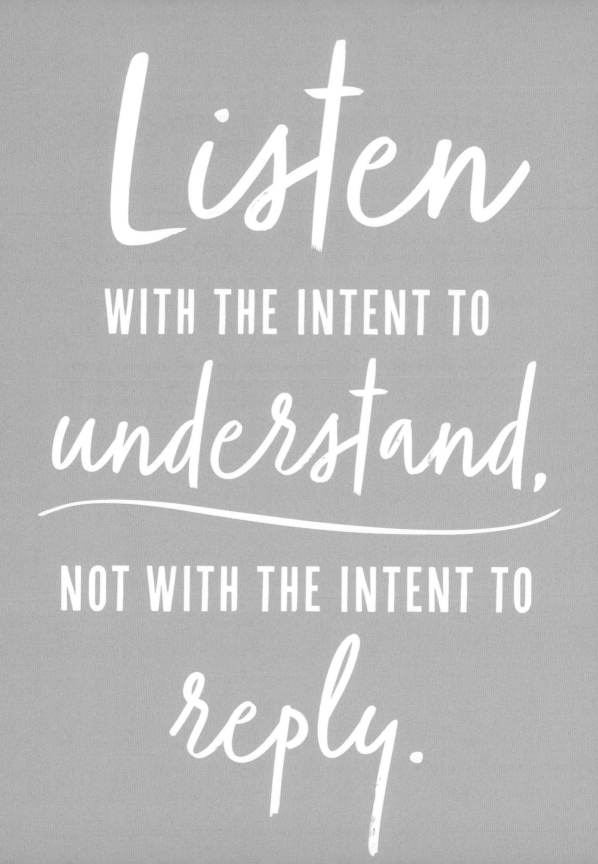

Tune Your Listening Skills

Having a dream team is meaningless if you are not open to receiving and processing feedback. I had an experience with a founder whom I was advising: I would share feedback, and she would completely dismiss it. It didn't just happen once; it happened all the time. I eventually let that relationship dissolve. And I remember feeling, "Wow. What a big missed opportunity for her." She had worked so hard to get me to be a formal advisor and then didn't take advantage of what I had to offer her. By the way, I'm not saying you need to agree with the feedback, but do be respectful and have a conversation or healthy debate about it.

LISTENING TIPS

- *Pay close attention to facial expressions and body language, which can convey more emotions than words.*
- *Don't interrupt.*
- *Listen with the intent to understand, not with the intent to reply.*
- *Ask open-ended questions.*
- *Repeat what you've heard in your own words to confirm understanding.*
- *Take notes, so you can refer back to what was said.*

A big part of listening is asking the right questions. The best way to learn is by understanding how people approach different situations, the frameworks they use, and what they've learned from prior experiences. It's not by asking them what they would do if they were you.

I had a mid-level manager approach me recently about a challenging time she was having with her employee. She briefed me on the situation and then asked, "What should I do?" A better question would have been: "Have you been through anything like this before? I would love to understand how you approached it and in hindsight what you learned from it." The latter question would have been more likely to open up a richer dialogue and would have provided insights and perspectives that would have helped her make the decision. It's YOUR decision to make.

So, when you're approaching any member of your dream team, think about how you phrase the question so that you get the most out of it. Open-ended questions provide for richer dialogue.

Open-ended questions start with:	*Closed-ended questions start with:*
◯ *How?*	◯ *Will?*
◯ *Why?*	◯ *Are?*
◯ *In what way?*	◯ *Is?*
◯ *Tell me more!*	◯ *Did?*
	◯ *Should?*

Here are a few of my favorite open-ended questions for different situations. (These can be applicable to your dream team and other colleagues as well.) Try them out and make them your own!

When you are in disagreement:

○ *Can you tell me more? I want to make sure I'm understanding your perspective.*

When you are at a crossroads and need to make a decision:

○ *Have you been in a situation like this before? How did you approach making your decision?*

When you are looking for feedback:

○ *What else should I be considering?*

When you are asking about an experience the person had in the past:

○ *What were your biggest insights from going through that experience?*

Asking

THE RIGHT
QUESTION CAN
INTRODUCE

possibilities

THAT YOU NEVER
KNEW EXISTED.

Be Specific with Your Asks

"Can I pick your brain?" is a networking phrase that needs to be retired. It not only conjures a less-than-desirable visual, but it also leaves the other person feeling as if there is no purpose or direction for the meeting. People inherently want to be helpful, but they also are protective of their time (as they should be!). Instead, be very specific with your request for information or action.

When my friend Ajay started a new executive leadership role at a major global company, he sent an update email to his network and also included some very specific asks (in bullet points, nonetheless). He made it very easy for his "brain trust of friends and colleagues," as he described them, to follow through on the requests. He asked them to:

- *like/comment on his job announcement post on his LinkedIn update*
- *share any thoughts on new trends or strategies to increase his external visibility in the industry*
- *make introductions to peers who are doing awesome things in his same field or driving innovation in specific topics that he listed*

By being specific, Ajay was able to get so much value in return.

What do you need from your dream team?

Think about your RBGs and the important projects you're working on. How can your own brain trust help accelerate your goals? Write down some specific asks.

A Mentor's Perspective

I've had the privilege of mentoring hundreds of women across a wide spectrum from corporate to nonprofit to entrepreneurs. Here is what I appreciate as a mentor:

○ When a mentee is prepared for the meeting and has very specific challenges/questions --> shows respect for my time

○ When a mentee reaches out just to check in and see if she can be helpful --> shows that she is looking to build a mutually beneficial relationship

○ When a mentee amplifies a project or cause I care about on her social media channels --> shows thoughtfulness and consideration

○ When a mentee actively listens to and processes the feedback I'm giving --> shows respect for my opinions and experience

○ When a mentee is responsive with deliverables --> shows respect, period

Pause and Reflect

I've shared a lot of specifics on how to build a dream team, but, most importantly I hope what you take away from this section is that investing time, energy, and thoughtfulness into cultivating relationships is the best investment for your career. As you build your dream team, don't get overwhelmed by assembling a "perfect" personal board of advisors. Your dream team will ebb and flow and evolve as you evolve. They will cheer you on, be a sounding board, and challenge you to achieve big things. When we support each other, incredible things happen. You're almost done with this book! The final step is to reflect and reset.

Meditation

Take a moment to scan your body for any tension that you might be feeling and see if you can soften any tightness that is there.

In this meditation, we'll reflect on our connection with others. As we move in the direction of our dreams, being present for others and building our network of personal and professional relationships is key. This takes awareness, time, and energy.

We purposefully choose people who we will cherish and support and those who will help us achieve our goals with new skills and confidence. We care deeply for one another.

When we're distracted with everyday tasks and to-do lists, we may forget to build and nurture this important network.

Our relationships are the foundation we build upon as we move through different phases in our lives. When we bring ourselves more fully to our relationships, with kindness and compassion, we feel the power of authentic connection. This creates lasting trust and encourages people to be their best selves.

As you end this reflection, look for opportunities to show up for others. Invite yourself to be a more active listener and to form genuine connections with the people you choose.

 If you would prefer to listen to the meditation, scan the QR code or visit franhauser.com/loveyourcareer.

Musings, Downloads, and Doodles

Reflect and Reset

As you reach for those RBG milestones, my hope is that you are feeling anchored by knowing your value and being supported by your dream team.

This last section is about how to move mindfully through your career with clarity, intention, and confidence. It's about being purposeful and about recognizing the importance of doing the work—of embracing the work—every single day to actively create the career of your dreams.

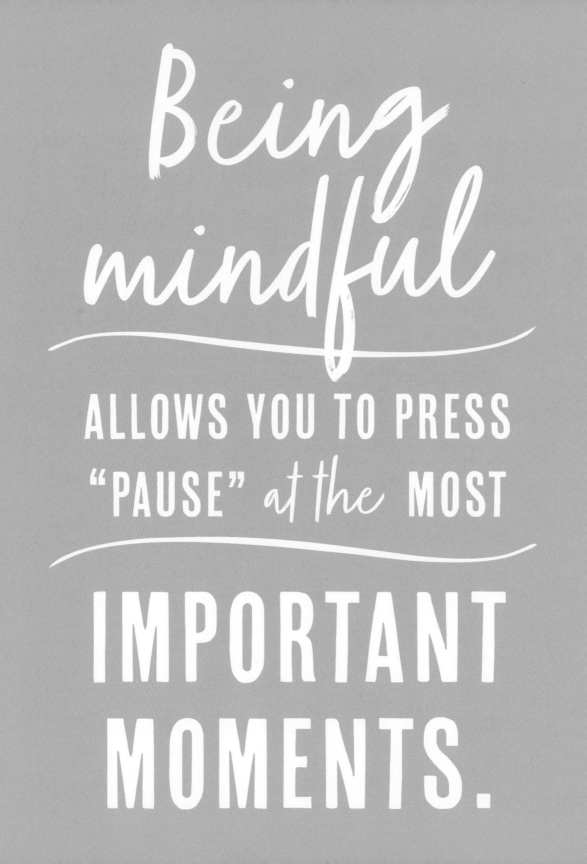

Being *mindful* ALLOWS YOU TO PRESS "PAUSE" at the MOST IMPORTANT MOMENTS.

Mindfulness Matters

Y ou know when you have those times in your life where you are on autopilot or maybe spinning out of control? We've all had them. It doesn't feel good. Now think about a time where you were able to control the way that you reacted to a difficult situation or were able to focus on a task for an hour to make great progress. This is the benefit of mindfulness. Being mindful helps you enjoy the process (or at least get through a difficult situation in a way that you can feel good about), and it helps you achieve a more productive outcome.

For me personally, being mindful allows me to move through my career and life with intention. When I'm mindful, I feel as if I am calling the shots versus letting life happen to me.

How does mindfulness play into achieving your RBGs? Being mindful will help you be great at your job, build relationships, deepen your skills, and present yourself in an authentic way.

When you're mindful:

○ *you are able to get out of the weeds and focus on the bigger picture (i.e., your RBGs)*

○ *you are able to make deeper connections with people by truly being present and by actively listening, engaging, and being empathetic*

○ *you are able to focus on doing the work and mastering a skill*

○ *you are able to be clear on who you are and how you present yourself to the world (i.e., your brand)*

Also, since your RBGs can evolve and change, mindfulness helps you find those quiet, thoughtful moments to check in on your career journey and reset and adjust.

Less rumination

Better working
memory

Better focus and
attention

*Benefits of
Mindfulness*

Less stress and
anxiety

Regulated
emotions

Integrating Mindfulness into Your Career Journey

So, if you've bought into the idea that mindfulness matters, you might be thinking, "How do I make this happen?" What's great about mindfulness practices is that they don't have to take up a huge amount of your time. I have three practices that I've integrated into my day that allow me to be more clear, intentional, and confident as I'm realizing my goals. They are:

1 *pressing "pause"*

2 *grounding myself with a morning ritual*

3 *making time to connect*

These are examples of how I practice mindfulness every day to stay connected to my purpose. Try them yourself or use them as inspiration to design your own!

1. PRESS "PAUSE" (AGAIN)

In the Say "No" section on page 83, we talked about the importance of pausing before you give that knee-jerk "Yes." Pausing is also powerful when it comes to your reaction to a difficult situation. Emotional energy and output can consume just as much of your time and energy as unnecessary tasks and to-dos.

When you're having a conversation with someone who is disagreeing with you or "pushing your buttons" in some way, stop and take a breath before you respond. I've found myself in situations where even after doing that, I knew that I needed to walk away and then come back to the conversation. It was pretty clear to me that I wouldn't be able to participate in a healthy, productive conversation. It's totally fine for the pause to be longer than a few seconds. You might have to ask the person if you can sit with it and pick up the conversation in the morning.

So much of this is about being aware of your visceral reactions and choosing not to respond when you are experiencing those reactions. Whether it's in person, on email, or via social media, choosing to sit on it will help you take the emotional reaction off the table and have a professional conversation.

Can you identify your visceral reactions to a trigger? It may be a knot in your stomach, a tension in your throat, or a tightening of your jaw. Another way to think about it is to ask yourself whether you tend to go into fight, flight, or freeze. How does that manifest for you? Be aware of these physical sensations and, when you feel them, consciously choose not to take any action at that moment.

Identify and write down some of the ways that you react in a difficult situation. Being aware of these and making a mindful decision to NOT react can save a lot of agita down the road!

2. GROUND YOURSELF WITH A MORNING RITUAL

My morning ritual is the first thing I do after I have a glass of water. I sit down on my comfy couch in prayer position and thank God for this beautiful day. (It doesn't matter if it's yucky out; I always start with those words.) Then I might ask her for help with something I'm struggling with ("Please help me be more self-assured") and ask her to look over people in my life who are in pain. I do a short meditation (one minute or so) and then write down three things I'm grateful for. The whole exercise (prayer, meditation, gratitude) takes less than five minutes, grounds me for the morning routine with my kids, reminds me of my purpose, and puts me in a positive frame of mind for the rest of the day.

For the meditation part of my ritual, I love the Meditation Studio app. (Their guided meditations are short and inspiring.) But I also know that meditating can be really hard for some people. Another option is a deep breathing practice like the starfish or five-finger method: Start with your pinky and trace your fingers up and down, breathing in on the up, and out on the down. When you breathe deeply, it sends a signal to your brain to relax, which then sends a message to your body to do the same.

"BREATHING IN,
I CALM MY BODY.
BREATHING OUT,

I smile."

— Thich Nhat Hanh

Create your own five-minute ritual

Make this your own. The power is in the habit, not when you're doing it or what you're doing during this time. For a little inspiration, here is a menu of practices that you can pull from to create your own mindfulness ritual.

○ Stand and ground your feet to the floor (feel your connection to the earth); take three deep breaths.

○ Do a simple stretch (standing, seated, or lying down).

○ Breathe in your favorite essential oil.

○ Write down a few things you are grateful for.

○ Reflect on something nice you did for someone.

○ Say a short prayer.

○ Do the five-finger breathing method (see page 181).

○ Say a mantra. My favorite is: "Breathing in, I calm my body. Breathing out, I smile." You can make up your own!

○ Read an affirmation that grounds you. (You will choose your favorite on page 186.) One of my favorites is: "My thinking is peaceful, calm, and centered."

Tip:

Create a comfy spot for your practice and leave everything you need there (whether it's a gratitude journal, an essential oil, etc.). Make it easy for yourself!

✏️ *Create your own mindfulness ritual.*

3. MAKE TIME TO CONNECT

Work can feel very transactional at times. Do you ever go into a work or even a personal conversation focusing only on what you need to get out of it? Especially when you're busy? You might be saying to yourself: "I have thirty minutes with this person, and I need to make sure that I walk away with A, B, and/or C." Sometimes I find myself jumping right in instead of asking the other person how they are doing and genuinely showing an interest in them. You know what I've realized over time? Taking two minutes at the beginning of a conversation to actually see and listen to the other person will make the remaining twenty-eight minutes so much more productive and meaningful. If you know that the person is struggling with a certain part of the project, ask them how it's going. Or bring up something from your last conversation so they feel heard and that you care.

One way to make sure that you take the time at the beginning of the conversation to connect is to build transition time into your calendar in between meetings. This way, you can take a few minutes to collect your thoughts and get grounded.

Tip:

Review your calendar for upcoming meetings to make sure you have transition time built in.

Reflect: Choose an Affirmation to Help You Love Your Career

Throughout this book, I've shared some of my favorite affirmations. Affirmations can change your pattern of thinking and inspire you to reach your goals. Now it's time to pick your favorite or write your own if you're feeling inspired! What could be your guiding affirmation—whether it's one that jumped out to you from these pages or a new personalized one—to help you love your career? Below is a list of the affirmations that appeared in the book. Circle the one that stands out to you and, when you need a boost, read it and repeat it.

○ *You are deserving of a career you love.*

○ *Honest self-reflection will open doors that you never knew existed.*

○ *Your network is your lifeline.*

○ *You have the power to create your own opportunities.*

○ *What do you want to be known for?*

○ *There is beauty in the process of achieving, failing, and resetting.*

○ *Create time in your day for the things that matter or bring you joy.*

○ *Saying "No" can be the best form of self-care.*

○ *I'm actually as proud of the things we haven't done as the things we have done.*

○ *Good enough is better than perfect.*

○ *If you take a risk and it doesn't go as planned, welcome to the club.*

○ *Self-assurance is a skill you develop by paying close attention to your successes in life and how you accomplished them.*

- You are not alone.
- Your dream team will ground you when you're lost and inspire you when you're stuck.
- Listen with the intent to understand, not with the intent to reply.

- Asking the right question can introduce possibilities that you never knew existed.
- Being mindful allows you to press "pause" at the most important moments.
- Breathing in, I calm my body. Breathing out, I smile.

If you want to take a crack at creating your own, here are some thought starters:

I am capable of

My thinking is

I live my

My world is

My impact is

I am at my best when

Your go-to affirmation:

Pause and Reflect

Mindfulness can feel like a buzzword, but the reason everyone talks about it is because being mindful makes things easier. In fact, being mindful can create more time for you—it's true! When you're thoughtful about your actions and reactions, and when you schedule time to connect with yourself and others, you actually triple your impact and output. Deep thoughts lead to deep work. Taking an extra moment helps you focus, visualize what will make you love your career, and achieve your RBGs. And that's all because you took a moment to reflect. Reflection can lead to change—often even a change in your previously set goals or desires. That's okay; that's amazing, in fact. I hope that this book inspires action and that you continue to revisit it often. The more time you spend embracing the work, the more you will fall in love with your career.

Meditation

When we choose to be mindful, we are making the all-important choice to be still and to ground ourselves in the present moment.

Mindfulness tools teach us to place our awareness on our *intention*, *attention*, and *attitude*. When we do this, our approach to almost anything, especially how we show up for ourselves and others, becomes crystal clear.

You can set your intention for how you want to show up for others or what you want to achieve or even *who you want to be*. Will your intention be to pause before responding in difficult conversations? To show up with confidence? To be kind to yourself in any situation? To listen deeply to your friends and colleagues? Take a moment to set one or more intentions for yourself.

When you have a clear intention, you can focus your attention more purposefully.

And next, you can choose the attitude that you want to cultivate. Will you be patient and kind? Generous? Will you have an attitude of curiosity versus judgment?

Mindfulness gives us the tools to be in the present moment with an open, curious, and kind mind. We can choose to let go of nagging thoughts that don't support our intention, attention, and attitude. This brings us into alignment.

As this meditation comes to a close, I invite you to remember these three ideas: What is my intention? Where will I place my attention today? What attitude do I hope to cultivate?

If you would prefer to listen to the meditation, scan the QR code or visit franhauser.com/loveyourcareer.

Musings, Downloads, and Doodles

Final Thoughts

You made it! I hope you found this book as fun and inspirational to go through as I found writing it to be. I also know that some of these questions may have challenged you in ways you hadn't expected. They did that for me, too. Taking the time—even if it was just for a few moments—to visualize your career happiness and consider your answers is an incredible accomplishment.

I hope that you can clearly see the amazing progress you've made. And keep that word in mind: *progress*. That's the goal here. There should be no pressure on this being "final"—it's a work in progress. I hope this book helped add clarity to your thoughts and intentions and that you come back to it often.

Keep in mind that you already had the traits and strengths to be successful inside of you. And where there are small gaps, you have a team of awesome people to support you.

Dream big, embrace the work, and love your career!

P.S. I've added a couple of shortcuts in the Love Your Career Tool Kit (page 197) to help move you into action!

Love Your Career Tool Kit

In this section you'll find some tools that will help you define clear next steps and remind you to check in periodically so you can stay on track. You will also find extra Career Action Plan worksheets.

Quick Start

If you're feeling overwhelmed or not sure where to begin, here is a short list of very doable next steps:

	Next Steps	Page #
☐	Go back and look at your notes from sections 1 and 2. Knowing what you know now, is there anything you would change? If so, update those sections now.	9
☐	Make your Career Action Plan accessible and visually stimulating. What works best for you: writing in the section at the back of this book or using the digital download? Do you want to cut out your plan and put it up on a bulletin board? Or would you rather flag the page in this book?	64
☐	Write your "kind 'No'" and save it as a canned email response in your drafts folder.	90
☐	Make the first entry into your Smile File. Any recent positive feedback or congratulatory emails you can add?	125
☐	Create a morning ritual. Even if it's just lying in bed staring at the ceiling for three minutes before you reach for your phone.	183
☐	Keep it up! Set a recurring appointment on your calendar for your regular check-in.	🙌

Love Your Career Check-In

Life gets busy. To make sure I'm being proactive and not just reactive with my priorities, I allocate an hour once a week (I usually do this on Fridays) to check in on my successes and setbacks. I ask myself, "What worked well?" and "What distracted me?" Use this checklist to reflect on your progress and keep your career dreams on track. Choose a recurring time that works for you—weekly, monthly. What's important is that you create a habit of reflection.

 Review your RBGs. *Are there any you can cross off the list because you've accomplished them? (Yay!) As you've been opening your eyes and listening to the world, do you have any changes you'd like to make? Any new learning, connecting, or branding opportunities? Write down your revised RBGs in your Career Action Plan.*

Check in on time management. *Look closely at your calendar and to-do list. Are your appointments and to-dos aligned with your RBGs? If not, adjust your schedule and begin to say "No" or delegate some requests.*

Add to your Smile File. *If you haven't written anything down in your Smile File this week, take this opportunity to add a few things that have made you proud. It could be a successful outcome, the way you handled a difficult situation, or even an insight that will help you in the future.*

Reflect on where you may need help. *Are you feeling stuck? Do you have a decision that you're struggling with? Who on your dream team can you reach out to to be a thought partner for you?*

Appraise your mindfulness. *Give yourself space to reflect on how you're doing with your mindfulness practices. What's working for you, and what isn't? Is there a new practice that you'd like to try? Remember, everything should be fluid.*

Digital download available at franhauser.com/loveyourcareer

Career
Action Plan

Use these extra pages any time you'd like to update your Career Action Plan. If you prefer a digital download, visit my website at franhauser.com/loveyourcareer.

Career Action Plan

Area	RBG	Next Step
Value Creation		
Connections		
Skills		
Brand		

Career Action Plan

Area	RBG	Next Step
Value Creation		
Connections		
Skills		
Brand		

Career Action Plan

Area	RBG	Next Step
Value Creation		
Connections		
Skills		
Brand		

Career Action Plan

DATE: / /

Area	RBG	Next Step
Value Creation		
Connections		
Skills		
Brand		

Career Action Plan

DATE: ___ / ___ / ___

Area	RBG	Next Step
Value Creation		
Connections		
Skills		
Brand		

Career Action Plan

Area	RBG	Next Step
Value Creation		
Connections		
Skills		
Brand		

Career Action Plan

Area	RBG	Next Step
Value Creation		
Connections		
Skills		
Brand		

Career Action Plan

DATE: /   /

Area	RBG	Next Step
Value Creation		
Connections		
Skills		
Brand		

Career Action Plan

DATE: /   /

Area	RBG	Next Step
Value Creation		
Connections		
Skills		
Brand		

Career Action Plan

DATE: /   /

Area	RBG	Next Step
Value Creation		
Connections		
Skills		
Brand		

Career Action Plan

Area	RBG	Next Step
Value Creation		
Connections		
Skills		
Brand		

Career Action Plan

DATE: / /

Area	RBG	Next Step
Value Creation		
Connections		
Skills		
Brand		

Career Action Plan

DATE: / /

Area	RBG	Next Step
Value Creation		
Connections		
Skills		
Brand		

Acknowledgments

This book came together very quickly (from concept to launch in one short year!). I'm so grateful to everyone who bought into my vision and mobilized to help me make it a reality.

First off, thank you to the beta readers who provided feedback on everything from the title to the topics and exercises covered in the book. Your feedback made the book so much better. Thank you: Agata Wlodarczyk, Alice Yang, Ari Weiss Saft, Daejauna Donahue, Jackie Reef, Dr. Jane Sojka, Jennifer Scott Mobley, Joy Sybesma, Julie Stewart, Kim Dao Phan, Lauren Busch, Lauren Matthews, and Michelle Edwards.

When I was working on launching my first book, *The Myth of the Nice Girl*, a group of women came together to help me promote it. The Nice Girl Army is now made up of over 150 amazing women who embody the concept of women supporting women. They are a constant source of encouragement, feedback, and action. Love you, ladies.

I'm so grateful to my agents at All American Entertainment, Maddy McPeak and Sarah Miller. Corporate sales are critical with this kind of book, and their enthusiasm and smart go-to-market strategy means everything.

I can never express enough gratitude to one of my dearest friends, Patricia Karpas. Patricia is a mindfulness advisor and wrote the meditations in the book. She has a knack for finding the perfect words that help us to pause and reflect. I felt it was important to build these reset moments into the book and she came through in spades.

This book would not have happened without Kathleen Harris. I asked Kathleen to help me line-edit the book. Our work together turned into so much more. She really made the book come to life and helped me make some important structural decisions. I've had the privilege of working with Kathleen for the past four years and feel truly blessed to have her as a partner.

Thanks to the incredibly talented and supportive team at The Collective Book Studio, including Angela Engel, Amy Treadwell, AJ Hansen, Chris Hemesath, David Miles, Dean Burrell, Elisabeth Saake, Ella Gilbert, and Regina Shklovsky. Angela is the kind of entrepreneur that, in my day job as an investor, I love backing—she's innovative, smart, and tenacious and I'm so grateful that she saw the opportunity with this book.

My family is a constant source of inspiration to me. I'm so grateful to my husband, Frank, and my sons, Anthony and Will, for giving me the space and encouragement to create. Hearing "you got this, Mom" never gets old. I love you all to pieces.

To each and every friend and colleague who has inspired me along the way. Your generosity with your insights, time, energy, and so much more, will always be remembered.

Photo credit: Jennifer Mullowney

About the Author

Fran Hauser is an author, keynote speaker, and start-up investor. She is passionate about helping women build fulfilling careers and successful businesses. Fran has invested in more than twenty-five female-founded companies across consumer packaged goods, media and publishing, and wellness. Her writing, speaking, and investing is informed by fifteen years spent in media, where she rose through the ranks at Time Inc. to become the president of digital. She is the best-selling author of *The Myth of the Nice Girl: Achieving a Career You Love without Becoming a Person You Hate*, which has been translated into six languages and was named "Best Business Book of the Year, 2018" by Audible. Visit FranHauser.com.

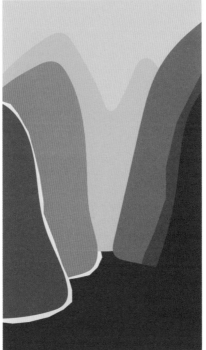